The
Spanish-American
War

HISTORICAL OVERVIEW
AND
SELECT BIBLIOGRAPHY

"The Birth of a Marine Giant"

NAVAL HISTORY BIBLIOGRAPHIES, NO. 5

The Spanish-American War

HISTORICAL OVERVIEW AND SELECT BIBLIOGRAPHY

Michael J. Crawford
Mark L. Hayes
and
Michael D. Sessions

Naval Historical Center
Department of the Navy
Washington
1998

Secretary of the Navy's
Advisory Subcommittee on Naval History

Pen and ink drawings by John Charles Roach

Library of Congress Cataloging-in-Publication Data

Crawford, Michael J.
    The Spanish-American War : historical overview and select
  bibliography / Michael J. Crawford, Mark L. Hayes, and Michael D.
  Sessions.
        p.   cm. — (Naval history bibliographies ; no. 5)
    Includes bibliographical references and index.
    ISBN 0–945274–40–8
    1. Spanish-American War, 1898—Bibliography. 2. Spanish-American
  War, 1898.   I. Hayes, Mark L. II. Sessions, Michael D.
  III. Title. IV. Series
  Z1243.C73   1998
  [E725]
    016.9738'6—dc21   98–39710

∞ The paper used in this publication meets the requirements for permanence established by the American National Standard for Information Sciences.

For sale by the U.S. Government Printing Office
Superintendent of Documents, Mail Stop: SSOP, Washington, DC 20402–9328

Contents

Supply ships depart San Francisco

Descriptive List of Illustrations

Foreword

The purpose of this publication is to encourage understanding and further study of the naval aspects of the Spanish-American War. Study of the sea services in this conflict is especially important because of the central role the Navy played in nearly every aspect of the war from logistics to diplomacy. American planners and leaders anticipated that the fight with Spain would be primarily a naval war. The U.S. Navy's victories at Manila Bay and Santiago de Cuba were pivotal events that turned the course of the war and America's future. Joint Army-Navy operations at Santiago, Puerto Rico, and Manila sealed the success won by the U.S. Navy's command of the seas.

This bibliography will prove useful for several reasons. The centennial of the Spanish-American War has brought forth a number of new articles and books on the conflict. Moreover, the compilers of this bibliography have included numerous older works, many published during or just after the war, but not listed in earlier bibliographies, and works in languages other than English. Readers will find here the most comprehensive listing available of works, conveniently grouped by topic, that touch on the naval war. Scholars seeking original avenues of investigation for themselves or for their students will do well to examine the section on needs and opportunities for research and writing.

In a collaborative work like this one, it is often difficult to assign due credit. In general, however, the authors divided responsibilities as follows: Captain Michael Sessions, USNR, as commanding officer of the Center's Reserve Volunteer Training Unit, VTU 0615, prepared the preliminary list of works. Dr. Crawford, head of the Center's Early History Branch, and Mark L. Hayes, a historian in that branch, edited the list, appended additional works, verified the entries for accuracy and appropriateness, and wrote the annotations. Mr. Hayes researched and wrote the historical overview and the section on needs and opportunities for research and writing.

Captain John Charles Roach, USNR, drew the original sketches found throughout the bibliography. Captain Roach took the time to research and draft these representations during the same period he was completing some 150 artworks illustrating the international peacekeeping mission in Bosnia as a member of the Joint Military History Office. His contribution to this publication is evidence of a deep commitment to his art and to naval history.

I join the authors in expressing the hope that this publication will be a valuable resource to anyone interested in the history of our nation and of the United States Navy.

WILLIAM S. DUDLEY
Director of Naval History

Preface

On 10 June 1898, one hundred years ago from the penning of this preface, Commander Bowman McCalla and Lieutenant Colonel Robert Huntington led a U.S. Navy and Marine Corps expedition into Guantánamo Bay, Cuba, in one of the most important actions of the Spanish-American War. The anchorage seized in this operation was crucial for the maintenance of a close blockade of Spanish warships at Santiago de Cuba, about forty miles to the west. In the histories of the war this event is often overshadowed by the larger battles of Manila Bay and Santiago de Cuba. Similarly, in the histories of the U.S. Navy, the much longer Civil War and World War II often overshadow the important transitional period at the end of the nineteenth century. As authors, we hope the centennial of the Spanish-American War and this publication will remind the public and scholars of the influential place the events of 1898 hold in American history.

We are grateful to our colleagues within the Center for various forms of assistance. Mrs. Jean Hort, Director of the Navy Department Library, and her staff helped ably with on-line computer searches and interlibrary loan requests, as well as retrieved numerous works from the rare book room and special collections. Historians on the staff of the Early History Branch, E. Gordon Bowen-Hassell, Charles E. Brodine, Jr., Christine F. Hughes, and Carolyn M. Stallings, assisted in verifying and in copy editing bibliographical entries. Dr. Edward J. Marolda, the Senior Historian, and Dr. Jeffrey G. Barlow, a historian in the Contemporary History Branch, read and commented on the preliminary draft of the historical overview.

We also deeply appreciate the contributions of scholars from outside who lent their expertise. Dr. John R. Hébert, senior specialist in Hispanic bibliography of the Hispanic Division of the Library of Congress, offered a long list of suggested bibliographic entries written in Spanish. Dr. James R. Reckner, of the Department of History at Texas Tech University, and member of the Secretary of the Navy's Advisory Subcommittee on Naval History, offered his criticisms and suggestions.

As grateful as we are for the valuable assistance we received in preparing this work, we accept sole responsibility for the contents.

MICHAEL J. CRAWFORD
MARK L. HAYES
MICHAEL SESSIONS

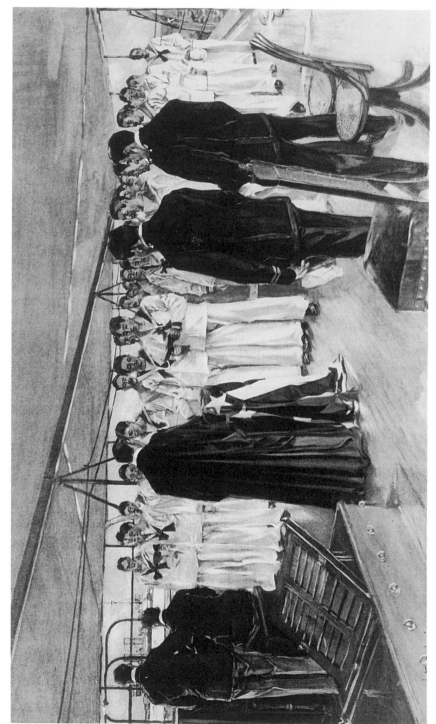

Sunday service on the battleship *Texas*

The
Spanish-American
War

ATLANTIC OCEAN

THE TROCHAS of CUBA

TAMPA

MIAMI

HAVANA

CIENFUEGOS

MANZANILLO

SANTIAGO de CUBA

C U B A

CARIBBEAN SEA

Historical Overview

Background and Preparation

The war that erupted in 1898 with Spain had its origins in the First Cuban Insurrection (1868–1878). The Cuban rebels had formed relationships with small groups of Americans committed to their cause. Many of these Americans supported the filibusters who attempted to run military supplies to the insurrectionists on the island. War had nearly erupted between the United States and Spain in 1873 when the Spanish captured the filibuster ship *Virginius* and executed most of the crew, including many American citizens. The Treaty of Zanjón signaled a temporary peace, but American sympathies remained with the Cubans desiring independence. When the reforms promised by the treaty proved illusory, the insurrectionists and their American supporters prepared for a new round.

Cuban emigrés in the United States formed clubs, raised money, and gained support from labor unions and the press. The movement also gained support in the Cuban business community following the depression of 1893 in the United States. The U.S. Congress responded to the economic crisis in part by raising tariffs on sugar imports from Cuba, plunging the island's export-dependent economy into a deep depression. Many Cuban businessmen blamed Spanish-American competition for their woes, and they thought that autonomy from Spain and closer economic ties with the United States would bring a return to prosperity. The military leaders of the new revolutionary army, José Martí, Máximo Gómez, and Antonio Maceo, began offensive operations on the island in April 1895. Martí announced that the war would be conducted by conventional means. However, when Martí died in an ambush soon after landing in Cuba, Gómez assumed command and decided to target the already battered sugar industry. Gómez believed that only an economic catastrophe would involve the whole island and force the Spanish to grant independence, as the cost of maintaining control became too great.

The Spanish government reacted by sending General Valeriano Weyler y Nicolau with orders to pacify the island. The "Butcher," as he became known in the United States, determined to deprive the rebels of support by forcibly re-concentrating the civilian population in the troublesome districts to areas near military headquarters. Nevertheless, military efforts alone were not enough to end the insurrection, and in Spain the Conservative government of Antonio Cánovas del Castillo was too weak to bring about meaningful reforms. Political opposition from Liberals, Carlists, and republicans, as well as the political influence of the Spanish army, severely limited Cánovas's freedom of action. Any conciliatory moves toward Cuban independence, or even home rule, would likely give the Conservative government's various opponents an issue around which they all could rally.

Upon taking office in 1897, President William McKinley hoped to avoid entanglement in the problems in Cuba so that he could pursue his domestic agenda of continuing the U.S. economy's recovery from the depression. Although some individuals pushed for overseas economic and territorial expansion, they were in the minority and did not reflect the general mood of the country at the beginning of McKinley's term. During the first year of his presidency, most of the American public was content to passively support the cause of Cuban independence. Public opinion in the United States dramatically changed by his second year, influencing the president to reorder his priorities.

To challenge Spain effectively on the issue of Cuba, McKinley needed a strong Navy. The service that the new administration inherited in 1897 was in the midst of sustained growth and reform following twenty years of purposeful neglect. At the close of the American Civil War, the U.S. Navy had in commission more than 600 vessels. Nearly all of the new ships were wartime purchases, hastily constructed, or made from unseasoned timber. After the war, most were sold off or destroyed. In spite of international crises such as the *Virginius* Affair, contention with Great Britain over the *Alabama* Claims, and problems with France over a projected canal in Panama, the strength of the Navy continued to decline. By 1879, only 48 of the Navy's 142 vessels were available for immediate service, and these were obsolete wooden or old ironclad ships. Naval technology had stagnated in the United States, illustrated by the fact that there was not a single high-power, long-range rifled gun in the entire fleet. In 1884 the U.S. Navy's newest ships were wooden-hulled steam sloops built in the previous decade.

Modernization began in the early 1880s during the administration of President Chester A. Arthur. Rapid growth in overseas markets and a foreign policy aimed at U.S. control of communications across the isthmus of Central America drove the country toward naval expansion. Two years of debate on the nature of this expansion culminated with the Navy Act of 1883, authorizing the construction of the steel cruisers *Atlanta*, *Boston*, and *Chicago* and the dispatch vessel *Dolphin*. The American fleet that began with these greatly superior vessels came to be known as the New Navy. Congress continued the process by approving additional steel warships, including the New Navy's first armored ships, USS *Texas* and USS *Maine*.

It was during the administration of Benjamin Harrison (1889–1893) that the Navy's strategy began to change from defense and commerce protection to offensive fleet action. President Harrison called for the continued and rapid construction of modern warships and the acquisition of bases to maintain the U.S. fleet in foreign seas. He later urged Congress to authorize construction of battleships, giving support to Secretary of the Navy Benjamin F. Tracy's goal of making the U.S. fleet strong enough "to be able to divert an enemy's force from our coast by threatening his own, for a war, though defensive in principle, may be conducted most effectively by being offensive in its operations."

Tracy proved to be an excellent administrator, and he marshaled allies for his expansionist policies in both Congress and the Navy, including Captain Alfred Thayer Mahan. Mahan's involvement stemmed from his strong belief that government leaders played a crucial role in determining the growth or decay of a nation's sea power. Navalists around the world used his 1890 publication, *The Influence of Sea Power upon History, 1660–1783*, to promote naval expansion in their own countries. American navalists' work bore fruit with the Navy Bill of 30 June 1890, authorizing construction of three battleships later named *Indiana*, *Oregon*, and *Massachusetts*. Along with the battleship *Iowa*, authorized in 1892, this force formed the core of a new fleet willing to challenge European navies for control of the waters in the Western Hemisphere.

While civilian leadership and U.S. industry prepared the Navy materially for an offensive war, a new institution, the Naval War College, prepared the service intellectually. Founded in 1884 and placed under the direction of Commodore Stephen B. Luce, the War College contributed greatly to the professionalization of the U.S. Navy's officer corps at the end of the nineteenth century. By the 1890s the curriculum at the War College featured training problems in which students drafted plans for operations in the event of war with specific countries under particular circumstances. Beginning in 1894 the War College under the direction of its president, Rear Admiral Henry C. Taylor, and later special boards convened by the Secretary of the Navy, examined the possibility of war with Spain over trouble in Cuba. When such a conflict appeared unavoidable in early 1898, the Navy Department had a solid body of planning studies honed by four years of debate among its leading officers. Although the realities of war would force several modifications, many of the concepts laid out in the naval plans were implemented: a strong blockade of Cuba, support for the insurgents, operations against Spanish forces in the Philippines and Puerto Rico, and the formation of a squadron to operate in Spanish waters. Perhaps more important, nearly every plan called for the purchase or charter of merchant vessels to serve as auxiliary cruisers, colliers, and transports. Data on these vessels furnished in lists appended to the plans served as a basis for decision making in those crucial weeks before war.

By contrast, the Spanish were ill prepared to defend their overseas possessions from outside intervention. Their vessels stationed in Cuba and the Philippines were obsolete and intended only to help the colonial government put down insurrection. They were unable to defend themselves against the modern steel ships of the U.S. Navy. Spain possessed only one battleship, *Pelayo*, and this was an older vessel that had just been modernized. This ship and the armored cruiser *Carlos V* were not ready for action until after the war began. Only four armored cruisers were available to steam across the Atlantic, and these suffered severe material deficiencies. The 10-inch guns were missing from *Cristobal Colon*, and there was a shortage of ammunition for the already defective 5.5-inch guns on the Spanish cruisers.

The Spanish Minister of Marine, Segismundo Bermejo y Merelo, revealed a lack of strategic planning in the vague orders given to Admiral Pascual Cervera y Topete in command of a squadron of four armored cruisers and three torpedo boats. Bermejo simply instructed Cervera to proceed to Caribbean waters and defend Spanish possessions against American attack. The Spanish also lacked enough colliers properly positioned to help their ships replenish once they were across the Atlantic. In addition, inadequate stockpiles of coal and coaling facilities at the ports in Cuba and Puerto Rico severely limited Cervera's options and ability to operate in the Caribbean. In short, the Spanish did not adequately prepare their forces and bases to defend their overseas possessions in the face of a challenge at sea. Once war began with a well-prepared naval power, such as the United States, Spain's possessions were almost certain to be cut off from the home country.

Destruction of *USS Maine* and the Rush Toward War

The assassination of Prime Minister Cánovas on 8 August 1897 led to the return of the Liberals to power in Spain, the recall of General Weyler, and a promise to grant autonomy to Cuba. Nevertheless, the insurgent leadership, sensing victory, refused to accept anything less than independence, and the government's many political opponents made it impossible for reforms to go far enough to win over the Cuban people. When pro-Weyler forces in Havana instigated riots in January 1898, Washington became greatly concerned for the safety of Americans in the country. The administration believed that some means of protecting U.S. citizens should be on hand, and the Spanish government should be reminded of America's serious interest in seeing an end to the Cuban conflict. As a result, on 24 January, after clearing the visit with a reluctant government in Madrid, President McKinley sent the battleship USS *Maine* from Key West to Havana.

The battleship arrived on 25 January. Spanish authorities in Havana were wary of American intentions, but they afforded Captain Charles D. Sigsbee and the officers of *Maine* every courtesy. In order to avoid the possibility of trouble, the U.S. Navy captain did not allow his enlisted men to go on shore. Sigsbee and the consul at Havana, Fitzhugh Lee, reported that the Navy's presence appeared to have a calming effect on the situation, and both recommended that the Navy Department send another battleship to Havana when it came time to relieve *Maine*.

At 9:40 on the evening of 15 February, a terrible explosion on board the U.S. warship shattered the stillness in Havana harbor. Later investigations revealed that more than five tons of powder charges for the vessel's 6- and 10-inch guns had ignited, virtually obliterating the forward third of the ship. The remaining wreckage rapidly settled to the bottom of the harbor. Most of *Maine*'s crew were sleeping or resting in the enlisted quarters in the forward part of the ship when the explosion occurred. Two hundred and sixty-six American sailors lost their lives as a result of the disaster. Captain Sigsbee and most of the officers survived because their quarters were in the after portion of the ship.

Spanish officials and the crew of the civilian steamer *City of Washington* acted quickly in rescuing survivors and caring for the wounded. The attitude and actions of the Spanish allayed initial suspicions that hostile action caused the explosion, and led Sigsbee to include at the bottom of his initial telegram the cautionary phrase, "Public opinion should be suspended until further report."

The U.S. Navy Department immediately formed a board of inquiry under Captain William T. Sampson to determine the cause of *Maine*'s destruction. The board met in Havana on 21 February, and their investigation lasted four weeks. The condition of the submerged wreck and a lack of technical expertise prevented the board from being as thorough as later investigating groups would be. In the end, they concluded that a mine had detonated under the ship. The board did not attempt to fix blame for the placement of the device.

When the naval court's verdict was announced, the American public reacted with predictable outrage. Fed by inflammatory articles in the "Yellow Press" blaming Spain for the disaster, the public had already placed guilt on the Iberian government and called for the liberation of Cuba. Destruction of *Maine* did not cause the United States to declare war on Spain, but it served as a catalyst, accelerating the approach to a diplomatic impasse. The sinking of the ship and death of U.S. sailors rallied American opinion behind armed intervention. With the threat of war larger than ever, the United States government stepped up preparations.

At the beginning of March 1898 the fleet of the United States Navy consisted of five battleships, two armored cruisers, thirteen protected cruisers, six steel monitors, eight old iron monitors, thirty-three unprotected cruisers and gunboats, six torpedo boats, and twelve tugs. Noticeably absent from this list, however, were colliers, supply vessels, transports, hospital ships, repair ships, and the large number of small vessels necessary for maintaining an effective blockade of Cuba's numerous ports. As the Navy Department's war plans clearly indicated, the government needed to purchase or contract for scores of these auxiliary ships. Assistant Secretary of the Navy Theodore Roosevelt organized a Board of Auxiliary Vessels that used information in the department's war plans to prepare a list of suitable private craft which would meet the Navy's expanded needs. On 9 March, Congress passed a $50 million emergency defense appropriation bill, and the Navy Department began to acquire vessels. By the end of the war, the Navy had purchased or leased 103 warships and auxiliaries. Another twenty-eight ships, including lighthouse tenders and the vessels of the Fish Commission and Revenue Cutter Service, had been added from existing government organizations. After the war auxiliary vessels such as colliers, refrigerator ships, and distilling ships became a permanent part of the fleet.

Secretary Long formally organized the Naval War Board in March 1898 to advise him on strategy and operations. Initial members were Assistant Secretary Theodore Roosevelt, Rear Admiral Montgomery Sicard (who had just arrived from command of the North Atlantic Station), Captain Arent S. Crowninshield, and Captain Albert S. Barker. By May, Captain Alfred Thayer Mahan joined the organization. This body was soon reduced in size, though, since Roosevelt left to become a lieutenant colonel in the First Volunteer Cavalry Regiment, and the Navy Department reassigned Captain Barker to command USS *Newark*. Although it had no executive authority, the board exerted considerable influence on operations through its advisory capacity. In particular, Mahan's views often dominated. Following earlier war plans, the board recommended concentrating on Spain's outlying possessions with a close blockade of Cuba, giving the U.S. Army time to mobilize sufficient strength for land campaigns in Cuba and Puerto Rico.

While the Navy Department worked with the President and the War Department in developing strategy, Secretary Long began positioning naval units for the opening of hostilities. Much of the North Atlantic Squadron was already concentrated for winter exercises at Key West, Florida. The first colliers did not reach the fleet until 3 May, nearly two weeks after the blockade began. On 17 March the battleships *Massachusetts* and *Texas* were ordered to join the armored cruiser *Brooklyn* at Hampton Roads, Virginia, to form the Flying Squadron under Commodore Winfield Scott Schley. The protected cruisers *Minneapolis* and *Columbia* joined Schley's force before the war started. The squadron was organized to protect the U.S. coast against a sudden attack by the Spanish armored cruisers of Pascual Cervera's squadron, known to be concentrating in the Cape Verde Islands. The Navy Department recalled the protected cruiser USS *San Francisco* and Commodore John A. Howell from Europe. On 20 April, Howell assumed command of the newly formed Northern Patrol Squadron, which was responsible for the protection of the coast and coastal trade from the Delaware capes to Bar Harbor, Maine. Rear Admiral Henry Erben commanded the Auxiliary Naval Force with his headquarters on shore at New York City. This command consisted primarily of eight old iron monitors stationed at several U.S. ports.

On 25 February, Assistant Secretary Roosevelt sent a telegram to Commodore George Dewey commanding him to concentrate the ships of the Asiatic Station at Hong Kong. In the event of war he was to take his squadron and destroy the Spanish ships in Philippine waters. Dewey's command at Hong Kong consisted of the protected cruisers *Olympia*, *Boston*, and *Raleigh* and the gunboats *Concord* and *Petrel*. The Revenue Cutter *McCulloch* joined the force on 17 April, and the protected cruiser *Baltimore* arrived on 22 April. Dewey also prepared for future operations in a region without friendly bases by purchasing the British steamers *Nanshan* and *Zafiro* to carry coal and supplies for his squadron.

Anticipating a showdown with the Spanish fleet in the Atlantic theater, Secretary Long ordered the battleship USS *Oregon* to depart from its home port at Bremerton, Washington, on 7 March, to begin the first leg of a 14,700-nautical-mile journey to Key West. The gunboat USS *Marietta* made the battleship's voyage quicker and easier by arranging for coal and supplies in the South American ports along the way. *Oregon* arrived at her destination on 26 May fully ready for operations against the Spanish fleet.

Although President McKinley continued to press for a diplomatic settlement to the Cuban problem, he accelerated military preparations begun in January when an impasse appeared likely. The Spanish position on Cuban independence hardened, and McKinley asked Congress on 11 April for permission to intervene. On 21 April, the President ordered the Navy to begin a blockade of Cuba, and Spain followed with a declaration of war on 23 April. Congress responded with a formal declaration of war on 25 April, made retroactive to the start of the blockade.

Opening Moves

International law required that a blockade had to be effective to be legal. With the absence of colliers and the Atlantic Fleet divided between Key West and Hampton Roads, the American effort was initially limited to the north coast of Cuba between Cardenas and Bahia Honda, and Cienfuegos on the south coast. In the early light of 22 April, Sampson's fleet steamed from Key West across the Florida Straits and began the blockade. Sampson believed he could reduce the defenses of Havana by bombarding the Spanish fortifications one at a time, beginning from the west. However, Secretary Long, following the advice of the Naval War Board, which expected Cervera's fleet to deploy to the Caribbean, ordered him not to risk his armored ships unnecessarily against land fortifications. The Navy Department was considering occupying the port of Matanzas, garrisoning it with a large military force, and opening communications with the insurgents. Long wanted Sampson to keep his most powerful ships ready to escort the transports if McKinley should decide on an early army landing in Cuba.

By the morning of 23 April, the advance ships of the blockading fleet were off their assigned ports. Additional vessels reinforced them over the next several days. The U.S. Navy struggled during the first weeks of the war to assemble the logistical apparatus necessary to support the blockade. Ships had to keep steam up in their boilers to pursue unknown vessels as they came into sight. Until colliers were fitted out and sent south, most of the blockading ships were forced to return to Key West to coal. Fresh water and food were also in short supply during the early days of the war.

The blockade was monotonous duty broken only by the rare capture of a Spanish vessel or an exchange of gunfire with gunboats and shore batteries. A few actions were intense, such as the one at Cardenas on 11 May when Spanish gunboats drew the U.S. Navy gunboat *Wilmington*, the torpedo boat *Winslow*, and the Revenue Cutter *Hudson* deep into the harbor. Hidden Spanish batteries ambushed *Winslow*, severely damaging her, killing ten and wounding twenty-one of her crew. While under heavy fire, *Hudson* towed the torpedo boat out of the harbor as *Wilmington* covered the withdrawal with rapid fire against the Spanish guns.

The U.S. blockading forces also undertook operations to isolate Cuba from telegraphic communications to Madrid via Cienfuegos, Santiago, and Guantánamo. The most celebrated action of this type occurred on 11 May off Cienfuegos. Commander Bowman H. McCalla of the cruiser *Marblehead* organized a party and planned an operation to cut the underwater communication cables. Marine sharpshooters and machine gun crews in steam cutters poured a continuous fire into Spanish positions on shore, along with gunfire support from *Marblehead* and the gunboat *Nashville*, while sailors in launches dragged the sea floor with grappling hooks for the cables. The launch and cutter crews endured heavy Spanish fire for three hours and cut the two main telegraph cables (leaving a third, local line), and dragged the ends out to sea. Every member of this expedition was awarded the Medal of Honor.

Battle of Manila Bay

Secretary Long telegraphed Commodore Dewey at Hong Kong on 21 April informing him that the U.S. blockade of Cuba had begun and that war was expected at any moment. On 24 April, British authorities informed the commodore that war had been declared and he must leave the neutral port within twenty-four hours, since the United States was now a belligerent. Dewey also received a telegram from the Navy Department instructing him to proceed immediately to the Philippine Islands and begin operations against the Spanish fleet. The American squadron moved to Mirs Bay on the Chinese coast thirty miles east of Hong Kong to await a circulating pump for *Raleigh* and the arrival of Oscar Williams, the American consul at Manila, who would have the latest intelligence on the Spanish military forces. They spent two days drilling, distributing ammunition, and stripping the ships of all wooden articles (which could add to fire damage on board ship caused by enemy gunfire). Almost immediately after Williams arrived on 27 April, the American ships departed for the Philippines in search of the Spanish squadron.

In a meeting called by the governor general of the Philippines on 15 March, Rear Admiral Patricio Montojo y Pasaron, in command of Spanish naval forces in the colony, concluded that his squadron would be destroyed by the onslaught of the American ships. The Spanish squadron consisted of seven unarmored ships carrying thirty-seven heavy guns and weighing a total of 11,328 tons. Montojo's largest ship was made of wood. Dewey's command was much stronger, consisting of six steel vessels mounting fifty-three guns and displacing 19,098 tons. Four of these had armored decks. Montojo recommended fortifying the entrances to Subic Bay, northwest of Manila, and moving his ships there to await Dewey's attack. If the Americans bypassed Subic and anchored in Manila Bay, Montojo believed his ships could sneak up on them during the night and inflict some damage. The governor general agreed. However, Montojo did not track the progress of the work in Subic Bay.

With the declaration of war the Spanish admiral took his squadron into Subic Bay only to discover that the commander there still needed another six weeks to mount his guns on Isla Grande at the bay's entrance. On 28 April, Montojo learned that the Americans had left Mirs Bay bound for the Philippines. After calling a council of his captains, he returned with his ships to Manila. Seventeen guns, including nine obsolete muzzleloaders, guarded the two passages into the Manila Bay. The Spanish attempted to mine the main channel, but the water was so deep and the entrance so wide that neither mines nor shore batteries were an effective barrier to enemy ships passing through during the night. Of the more than 200 guns near the city of Manila, only twelve were breech-loaders positioned to fire out to sea. Montojo rejected the idea of fighting under the guns of the city because civilian structures would likely be hit by American fire. The Spanish decided to anchor their ships in the shallow waters under the guns of the Cavite arsenal, on a small peninsula seven miles southwest of Manila. Deeply pessimistic about his fleet's chances of survival, Montojo believed the position gave his men the best chance to escape from their vessels should they be sunk in the upcoming battle.

Consul Williams accurately reported that Montojo intended to fight his squadron while under the guns in Subic Bay, and Dewey sent two of his cruisers ahead to reconnoiter. Finding Subic Bay empty, and in defiance of the reports of mines in the channel, the Americans pressed on into Manila Bay during the night of 30 April. In the early morning hours of 1 May, the U.S. warships discovered the Spanish squadron near Cavite. Leaving his two auxiliaries in the bay guarded by *McCulloch*, Dewey formed his remaining ships into a line and steamed for the enemy force. The Spanish opened the battle at 5:15 a.m., firing at the oncoming American ships. Dewey steamed his squadron in an oval pattern along the five-fathom curve, pouring a heavy fire into the outgunned and obsolete Spanish force. The enemy replied with wildly inaccurate gunfire from their ships and two 5.9-inch guns at Sangley Point. The Americans scored critical hits on the larger Spanish warships, setting them ablaze. After nearly two hours of fire, Dewey ordered his captains to withdraw, acting on reports from the crew that his ships were running low on ammunition.

Dewey took his squadron five miles off Sangley Point and signaled his captains to come on board to report the condition of their ships. The commodore discovered that his squadron had sustained very little damage and that it had plenty of ammunition to continue the battle. After allowing the crewmen to enjoy a light meal, Dewey ordered his ships to re-engage the remnants of Montojo's shattered squadron. The Spanish admiral had pulled his surviving vessels into the shallow waters of Bacoor Bay behind Cavite to make a final stand. Hitting the Spanish ships in their new anchorage proved difficult for the larger warships, so Dewey ordered the gunboats *Concord* and *Petrel*, with their shallow draft, to finish off the enemy at close range. The garrison at Cavite raised a white flag at about 12:15, and the firing ended shortly thereafter.

Montojo's fleet was destroyed, suffering 371 casualties compared to only 9 Americans wounded. When official word of the magnitude of the U.S. Navy's victory reached the United States, nearly a week later, the American public heaped enthusiastic praises on Dewey and jubilant celebrations erupted throughout the country. However, 26,000 Spanish regulars and 14,000 militia garrisoned various points in the Philippine Islands, including 9,000 men at Manila. The U.S. squadron took control of the arsenal and navy yard at Cavite, and Dewey cabled Washington stating that, although he controlled Manila Bay and could probably induce the city to surrender, he needed 5,000 men to seize and hold Manila.

The Hunt for Cervera

Admiral Cervera had repeatedly warned the Spanish Ministry of Marine that his squadron would face certain destruction if sent to the Caribbean. Under orders, on 29 April he departed the Cape

Verde Islands with his squadron of four armored cruisers, towing three torpedo-boat destroyers, intending to steam for Puerto Rico. To search for the Spanish squadron, the U.S. Navy Department dispatched three fast former mail steamers, *Harvard*, *Yale*, and *St. Louis*, to the Caribbean. The vessels established a patrol line stretching from Puerto Rico and along the Leeward and Windward Islands. As long as Cervera's location remained uncertain, the U.S. fleet would be divided between Rear Admiral Sampson's North Atlantic Fleet based in Key West and Commodore Schley's Flying Squadron based in Hampton Roads; the former maintained the blockade of Cuba and the latter guarded the East Coast of the United States from a sudden descent by the Spanish cruisers.

Sampson correctly deduced that Cervera intended to make for San Juan, Puerto Rico, and determined to deprive the Spanish fleet of the defensive advantages of that port. Leaving his smaller ships to maintain the blockade of Cuba's northern ports, the American admiral embarked on an eight-day journey, plagued by the slow speed and mechanical unreliability of his two monitors. The American force arrived off San Juan early on 12 May. After a nearly four-hour bombardment of the Spanish works, Sampson broke off the engagement and returned to Key West, satisfied that Cervera's ships were not in San Juan.

The need to tow their fragile destroyers slowed the Spanish squadron's crossing of the Atlantic. As he approached the West Indies, the Spanish admiral dispatched two of these vessels to the French island of Martinique to gain information on American movements and check on the availability of coal. On 12 May, Cervera learned that Sampson was at San Juan. The Spanish admiral also discovered that the French would not sell him any coal. Driven by the need to refuel his ships and the desire to avoid combat with a superior American force, Cervera steamed for the Dutch harbor of Curaçao. He arrived there on 14 May only to be further disappointed when the expected Spanish collier failed to arrive, and the Dutch governor authorized the purchase of only 600 tons of coal. After considering his options, Cervera chose to sail his fleet to Santiago de Cuba where he arrived on the morning of 19 May.

With Sampson out of touch for long periods during his return from Puerto Rico, Secretary Long on 13 May ordered Commodore Schley's Flying Squadron to Charleston, South Carolina, in preparation to intercept the Spanish fleet. Further orders directed Schley to Key West and a meeting with Rear Admiral Sampson. The Navy Department believed that Cervera's most likely objective was Cienfuegos because of its rail connection to Havana. Therefore, after arriving in Key West on 18 May, Schley received orders to take his squadron, reinforced by the battleship *Iowa* and several smaller vessels, to Cienfuegos. On 19 May, after Schley's departure, the White House received an unconfirmed report that the Spanish ships had run into Santiago de Cuba. Upon receiving this information, Sampson instructed Schley to proceed to Santiago if he was satisfied that Cervera was not at Cienfuegos. Uncertainty over the Spanish squadron's whereabouts, the difficulty of observing ships in the harbor at Cienfuegos, concerns over coaling in open waters, and perhaps Schley's own ego led to erratic movements by the Flying Squadron not in keeping with Sampson's or the Navy Department's expectations. After numerous delays, Commodore Schley established a blockade off Santiago de Cuba on 29 May.

When Cervera arrived at Santiago de Cuba he discovered that the port had neither enough coal nor supplies to provision his ships for a long voyage. Armed with reports that the American fleet was closing in on his location, the admiral called a council of his captains on 24 May to consider taking the squadron to San Juan. The council decided that it was best to remain where they were, refitting the ships as much as possible and hope for a later favorable opportunity to leave. Cervera seemed to believe that the only function his squadron could now serve was that of a "fleet in being," and therefore that one harbor was as good as another to occupy while under blockade. He briefly reconsidered his decision on 26 May, but reports of American ships off the coast persuaded him to stay in Santiago de Cuba. With the arrival of the Flying Squadron on 29 May, the opportunity for an uncontested departure disappeared.

The Navy in the Campaign for Santiago de Cuba

McKinley and his advisors had originally intended to wait until the end of the rainy season to send a major land expedition to Cuba. But, with the Spanish squadron bottled up at Santiago, U.S. leaders saw an opportunity to strike a damaging blow to the enemy's military capability in the Caribbean. On 1 June, Secretary Long informed Sampson that 25,000 men under Major General William Shafter were preparing to embark for Cuba from Tampa, Florida, and that the North Atlantic Fleet should convoy the troops and assist a landing near Santiago. Meanwhile, Sampson took steps to tighten the blockade of Cervera's squadron.

At the onset of the campaign Sampson seized on the idea of sinking a vessel in the narrow channel leading to the harbor of Santiago. He intended to keep the Spanish ships from escaping until the Army could capture the city or assist the Navy in passing the forts and mines at the harbor entrance. The Naval War Board in Washington approved, and Sampson selected the collier *Merrimac*, commanded during the operation by naval constructor Richard Pearson Hobson. Hobson and seven volunteers took the ship into the channel during the early morning hours of 3 June. Gunfire from Spanish shore batteries shot away the vessel's steering gear and anchor chains, making it impossible for the Americans to sink the vessel in the proper location. Only two of the ten prepared scuttling charges went off, and *Merrimac* came to rest too far up the channel to pose a serious obstacle. The Spanish captured Hobson and his brave men.

This failure forced Sampson to rely on a close blockade to keep the Spanish squadron in port. The American ships would need a safe place to refuel much closer to Santiago than either Haiti or Key West. Coaling at sea was a difficult and lengthy process. As a result, Sampson sent Commander McCalla and USS *Marblehead* to reconnoiter Guantánamo Bay as a possible anchorage. McCalla's report was favorable, and on 10 June the First Marine Battalion under Lieutenant Colonel Robert Huntington landed and established a position on the east side of the outer harbor. This unit defeated Spanish troops in the area and held the site for coaling operations throughout the campaign.

Major General Shafter's troop transports departed Tampa on 14 June, rendezvousing with their Navy escorts the following day. The expedition arrived off Santiago on 20 June and began to disembark at Daiquiri, east of the city, two days later. In addition to providing escort for the convoy, Sampson's ships furnished fifty-two steam launches, sailing launches, whaleboats, lifeboats, and cutters to help move the soldiers and their equipment ashore. Shafter expressed deep appreciation for the Navy's assistance because there were too few boats on the Army's transports to disembark the expedition in a reasonable length of time.

Sampson's armored ships maintained a tight blockade of Santiago de Cuba, coaling from colliers in open water when the seas were calm and from colliers at Guantánamo Bay when the weather required it. On the morning of 3 July, Admiral Cervera attempted to break out of the American blockade, thus precipitating the Battle of Santiago de Cuba. Near the entrance to the bay that morning were the battleships *Texas*, *Oregon*, *Iowa*, and *Indiana*, the armored cruiser *Brooklyn*, and the armed yachts *Vixen* and *Gloucester*. Most of the battle was a running fight as the blockading vessels attempted to get up enough steam to stay with their quarry. Foul bottoms and poor-quality coal reduced the speeds of the usually swift Spanish cruisers. Ranges between the combatants were often in excess of 4,000 yards, greater than the American crews had trained for and longer than their new range finders could handle. In addition, radical turns in the early stages of the battle complicated the U.S. Navy's gunnery problem. Smoke from the weapons' brown powder and frequent mechanical failures further reduced the effectiveness of its gunfire. The battleships and *Brooklyn* generally registered hits when they were able to maintain a parallel or near parallel course with the Spanish cruisers for several minutes. Although only 1.29 percent of American shots hit their targets, the volume of fire proved sufficient to destroy or run aground all of Cervera's vessels. The destruction of the Spanish cruiser squadron at Santiago de Cuba freed President McKinley and the Navy Department to pursue other strategic options.

Global Strategy

In the years prior to the war, U.S. planners had never reached a consensus on the issue of deploying a squadron of warships to European waters. Although the Naval War Board had not originally planned such a deployment, the formation of the Spanish navy's Reserve Squadron resurrected the debate. Following the departure of Cervera's squadron to the Caribbean, the Spanish Ministry of Marine began to organize a second squadron under Rear Admiral Manuel de la Cámara y Libermoore, centered around the battleship *Pelayo* and the armored cruiser *Emperator Carlos V*. Although U.S. Navy leaders believed that this force would reinforce Cervera, they had considered it possible that the Spanish ships would head for the Philippines. Consequently, Secretary Long dispatched the monitors *Monterey* and *Monadnock* on a slow and hazardous voyage across the Pacific to reinforce Dewey's command at Manila. Long's actions were vindicated when Spain's Reserve Squadron departed Cadiz on 16 June and steamed into the Mediterranean bound for the Philippine Islands.

The Navy Department responded to the news of Cámara's deployment by ordering Rear Admiral Sampson to detail two battleships, an armored cruiser, and three auxiliary cruisers for departure to Europe if the strong Spanish force passed into the Red Sea. When the Reserve Squadron arrived at Port Said on 26 June, Washington decided to organize formally a force entitled the Eastern Squadron. The command, which was activated on 7 July under the leadership of Commodore John C. Watson, consisted of the battleship *Oregon*, the protected cruiser *Newark*, and the auxiliary cruisers *Yosemite* and *Dixie*. The Navy Department added the battleship *Massachusetts* on 9 July, the auxiliary cruiser *Badger* on

12 July, and the protected cruiser *New Orleans* on 17 July. The Navy also assembled six colliers and a refrigerator ship at Hampton Roads, Virginia, to support the Eastern Squadron's deployment. The Navy Department allowed news of the squadron's formation and its intended target to be widely circulated, hoping that such news would force Spain to recall the Reserve Squadron to Spanish waters.

Cámara ran into difficulty attempting to refuel his ships at Port Said. The Egyptian government refused to sell him coal or to allow the Spanish squadron to take on coal from its own colliers while in port. Forced out to sea, where bad weather prevented coaling, the Spanish admiral took his squadron through the Suez Canal into the Red Sea and began refueling on 7 July. This delay allowed the Spanish government an opportunity to reconsider Cámara's mission in light of the near certainty that American ships would enter Spanish waters. The Sagasta government recalled the Reserve Squadron to Cadiz, and Watson's deployment was held in abeyance for the time being.

Even though Spain no longer threatened Dewey's forces at Manila, the Navy Department was concerned that Germany might try to take advantage of the situation to increase her colonial possessions in the Pacific. Rear Admiral Sicard and Captain Crowninshield of the Naval War Board still wanted to send Watson to reinforce Dewey, but Captain Mahan dissented from this view. Meanwhile, Watson's ships were needed to support the expedition to Puerto Rico. By the time the Eastern Squadron was free to depart the Caribbean, peace negotiations were under way, and Watson's deployment was held back for good.

Closing Campaigns

The U.S. Navy provided escort and support for the Army's final two campaigns of the war. On the afternoon of 21 July, the lead forces for the invasion of Puerto Rico got under way from Guantánamo Bay. The battleship *Massachusetts* as well as *Dixie*, *Gloucester*, *Columbia*, and *Yale*, all under the command of Captain Francis J. Higginson, steamed for Puerto Rico with nine transports loaded with 3,500 U.S. Army troops. Originally planning to land east of San Juan at Playa de Fajardo, the expedition's commander, Major General Nelson A. Miles, instead directed the Navy to land his force on the island's south coast. The expedition arrived off Port Guanica on the morning of 25 July. Lieutenant Commander Richard Wainwright of *Gloucester* requested and received permission to send a landing party ashore. The men soon came under fire from the small Spanish garrison but held their position until the first Army troops secured the landing place. Wainwright also assisted the amphibious landing at Port Ponce on the 28th when he stole into the inner harbor the night before and gathered up a number of enemy barges for the Army to use.

In the Pacific, Dewey's success at Manila Bay prompted the McKinley administration to take several important steps to support his squadron. Besides the two monitors previously mentioned, Secretary Long dispatched the protected cruiser *Charleston* from San Francisco on 22 May, with orders to seize the strategically located Spanish island of Guam on the way to Manila. The authorities on Guam, unaware until the American warship arrived on 20 June that the war had even started, surrendered the island without a fight. The first troops intended for the Philippines, under the command of Brigadier General Thomas M. Anderson, departed from San Francisco three days after *Charleston* and arrived at Manila on 30 June. Two more groups, one with the expedition's commander, Major General Wesley Merritt, left for the Philippines during June. Before the end of the war, 10,844 U.S. Army officers and men had deployed to the Philippines. In July the United States annexed the Hawaiian Islands, completing the path of U.S. controlled territories to the western Pacific.

Meanwhile, Dewey brought the Filipino insurgent Emilio Aguinaldo to Cavite, hoping to learn more about the Spanish garrison and welcoming any support the Filipino rebels might provide by their operations against Spanish forces. However, Dewey and the American consuls in the Far East overestimated their ability to control the consequences of this action, which was complicated by Aguinaldo's expectation that the United States would support his demand for the colony's independence. By the time American forces were prepared to assault Manila in August, the potential problems of cooperating with the rebels had become apparent to Dewey and Merritt. The American commanders reached an oral agreement with the governor-general at Manila to surrender the city after a brief naval bombardment and infantry assault. On the morning of 13 August, the guns from the U.S. squadron opened fire and Merritt's troops went forward. After sharp fighting in some quarters the Spanish surrendered, allowing the Americans to occupy Manila; thus keeping the Filipino insurgents out of most sections of the city. The peace protocol had been signed between the United States and Spain on 12 August, but word of this did not reach Manila until four days later.

Lessons and Legacies of the War with Spain

The Spanish-American War proved to be an important learning experience for the U.S. Navy. When detailed official reports of the Battles of Manila Bay and Santiago de Cuba were analyzed, American naval leadership slowly accepted that its naval gunfire had performed badly. The practice of firing too quickly, the use of brown powder that created increasing clouds of smoke with every shot, and long and rapidly changing ranges all contributed to American hit rates of less than 3 percent. This performance inspired naval officers, like Lieutenant William S. Sims, to search vigorously for new techniques and technology to improve U.S. naval gunnery. The war demonstrated the need for large numbers of auxiliary craft, especially colliers. Despite the advocacy of the Office of Naval Intelligence, the Naval War College, and the U.S. Naval Institute for these types of craft, it was not until coaling problems were revealed in the cruise of the Great White Fleet in 1908–1909 that the Navy Department requested appropriations for Navy colliers.

Alfred Thayer Mahan concluded that it was difficult for a representative government like that of the United States to adhere to sound military principles if there was not an appreciation for them among the people or their leaders. Mahan therefore examined the war in his writings and sought to educate the American public and its leaders about the basic principles of strategic naval warfare. Nothing illustrates better Mahan's concerns than his discussion of the formation of the Flying Squadron to protect the Atlantic coast of the United States just prior to the start of the war. He was convinced that dividing the fleet was strategically unsound since it weakened the blockade of Cuba and reduced Sampson's margin of superiority over Cervera. Nonetheless, it was politically necessary since American businessmen and inhabitants along the coast demanded protection from a sudden attack by Spanish warships. After the war, Mahan worked to widen the influence of his ideas, even supporting the strengthening of coastal fortifications so that the growing battle fleet would be free to operate in accordance with his ideas.

Mahan also believed that the war demonstrated that the number of ships was just as important as the size of individual vessels in determining the composition of the main battle line. Mechanical problems, the need to refuel, and the friction of war often affected the American fleet operating in the Caribbean. Mahan wrote that naval planners should consider these factors rather than simply advocating the construction of a few very large battleships. Mahan further argued that the war demonstrated that monitors had no place in an offensive-oriented fleet. They were too unseaworthy to steam great distances under their own power, and their slow speed served to limit the mobility of the entire fleet.

The U.S. Navy's contribution to victory over Spain was tarnished by at least one postwar examination. The nature of the running fight at the Battle of Santiago de Cuba on 3 July made it difficult to apportion credit for the lop-sided victory. Sampson had been on his way to confer with Shafter when the battle began, leaving Schley in charge of the ships maintaining the blockade. While Sampson's initial report did not mention Schley, some journalists took the opportunity to exaggerate the latter's role in the battle. Upset by the growing controversy, Sampson formally complained in writing to Secretary Long that Schley's conduct while hunting Cervera's squadron in May was "reprehensible." Sampson's letter became public during debate that followed President McKinley's proposal to make permanent Sampson's and Schley's promotions to rear admiral. Naval officers, congressmen, and newspaper editors lined up behind either Sampson or Schley as the controversy continued to grow. Neither the passage of the promotions on 3 March 1899 nor Secretary Long's circular the following November prohibiting officers from discussing the matter in public ended the damaging debate.

Hoping to put the issue to rest, Long eventually ordered Admiral of the Navy George Dewey to convene a court of inquiry to investigate the charges related to Schley's conduct. The court met for forty days beginning on 12 September 1901. In the final report a majority of court members were critical of Schley, but Dewey issued a separate opinion supportive of Schley's conduct. Neither Sampson nor Schley was satisfied by this turn of events, and both sides filed appeals as the public debate continued. When the judge advocate upheld the court's findings, Schley appealed directly to President Roosevelt in January 1902. Roosevelt, who saw the issue as a review of McKinley's decision to promote Sampson over Schley in 1899, supported the action of his predecessor, and the advocates now continued their fight through memoirs and historical narratives. The Sampson-Schley controversy discredited the otherwise excellent reputation of the U.S. Navy during the war and probably obstructed attempts to record an objective view of events. Participants who wrote accounts of the campaign and Battle of Santiago de Cuba in the years following the war could not help but be influenced by the controversy raging around them.

Aftermath

Although the Spanish-American War lasted fewer than five months, it had a lasting influence on the United States and signaled a dramatic change in its position in the world. It also marked the emergence on the global stage of the U. S. Navy.

The United States went to war with Spain in April 1898 to secure Cuban independence and end the revolutionary war that was killing thousands of Cuban civilians and damaging U.S. economic interests. As a result of the war, the United States became a world power by acquiring the Philippines, Guam, and Puerto Rico from a defeated Spain. Recognizing the need to support its new overseas interests, the country acquired through purchase or treaty the Hawaiian Islands, Guantánamo Bay, the Virgin Islands, and part of the Samoan archipelago.

Ironically, in winning a war against European colonialism, the United States became a colonial power itself and ended up suppressing, by force, a bitter insurrection in the Philippines. A major departure from American tradition, the acquisition of overseas colonies (especially the Philippines) stimulated a great national debate. Those opposed saw colonialism as a denial of America's high moral position in entering the war to win Cuba's freedom. They feared the consequences of an enlarged military establishment and foreign entanglements. Expansionists, on the other hand, saw the Philippines as a base for American trade in the Far East and as part of a campaign to ensure national greatness. The domestic market could not absorb all the output of American factories, and American farmers sought new markets for their agricultural surpluses. Protestant churches saw an opportunity to send missionaries to the Philippines to work among the population. Social Darwinists believed the United States had a duty to bring civilization, and what they considered to be a superior culture, to the native populations of the newly occupied territories. Navalists held that the United States could only hold its place and advance its interests in the world if the country had a strong navy; and a strong navy required a healthy merchant marine, overseas commerce, and naval bases and coaling facilities throughout the world.

The acquisition of overseas territories, along with memory of the Navy's victories in the Spanish-American War, led to the realization of Mahan's goals of a larger and more powerful fleet. The American people then viewed the Navy with greater understanding and even affection. Pictures of ships on stereo cards and sailor-suits for children became an indelible part of popular culture at the turn of the century. The Navy also benefited from the interest of President Theodore Roosevelt, a former Assistant Secretary of the Navy and an accomplished naval historian. Congressional appropriations in the next two decades provided for an unprecedented level of new construction, not only of warships, but also of auxiliary vessels necessary to maintain a fleet on deployments throughout the world.

Institutional changes also helped keep the Navy efficient. Naval administrators sought to make conditions of service attractive to young, native-born, American men. The amalgamation of the Engineer Corps with the Line in 1899 resolved a long-standing cause of dissension. Establishment of the Chief of Naval Operations in 1915 prepared the Navy Department to direct naval operations in the coming world war.

In short, the Spanish-American War was primarily a naval war, and the U.S. Navy was dramatically affected by the experience. Following the war, naval expansion continued at such a high rate that the Navy went from ranking sixth in the world in 1897 to being afforded equal status with Great Britain by the Washington Naval Treaty of 1922. The Spanish-American War served as a catalyst propelling the New Navy forward, preparing it to fulfill the country's added responsibilities as a major world power in the twentieth century.

"The little crew left them a mass of flames."

Needs and Opportunities for Research and Writing

The large number of books published on Spanish-American War topics illustrates that, even though it was one of America's shortest wars, it played a major role in the history of the United States. Many works have focused on the diplomatic aspects of the conflict, and much of the scholarship on the period has been directed at explaining the transition of the United States from a continental to a world power. General histories of the war are plentiful, and works by and about journalists abound. Naval operations seem to be well covered, but nearly all accounts lack the depth and analysis found in operational histories of other periods. The historiography of the war needs a modern history of naval operations that incorporates the impact of such issues as logistics, naval engineering, gunfire technology, mechanical unreliability, and crew training.

Perhaps the largest gap in the historiography of the early years of the New Navy is a study of the enlisted force. The period is known for the growing professionalization of the officer corps, but often overlooked is the Navy's development of a body of skilled, experienced petty officers in a service increasingly dominated by rapidly growing technology. Frederick Harrod in his excellent book, *Manning the New Navy: The Development of a Modern Naval Enlisted Force, 1899–1940*, provides a sketch of the early years as a context for his larger study. His focus is on the period following the Spanish-American War, when the sudden growth of the Navy demanded major changes in recruiting, organizing, and training the service's enlisted force. Many issues remain largely unexplored, such as how men, recruited under the system and standards of the days of wooden warships, trained and coped with the complex machines of the New Navy. A significant source of trained manpower during the war was the state naval militias, organizations similar to the National Guard. Many of these men were distributed throughout the fleet at the start of the war. However, four auxiliary cruisers were, with the exception of the captain, executive officer, and navigator, entirely manned by the naval militias of Massachusetts, New York, Maryland, and Michigan. The stories of these unique organizations and their men need telling.

Other subjects are also open to further research. William T. Sampson and Winfield Scott Schley, for example, stand among a number of naval personalities from the war who await full-length biographies. A detailed modern assessment of the Sampson-Schley controversy, including the role played by the American media and how the controversy affected the Navy is also needed. The historiography of the war needs a detailed examination of the administration of the Navy and its bureau system and an assessment of Secretary Long's leadership. The acquisition and role of hospital ships, colliers, transports, and other auxiliary vessels also deserve closer examination by historians.

The naval history of the Spanish-American War could serve as the basis for several comparative studies. For example, a deeper understanding of the development of naval gunfire technology and techniques could be achieved by a comparative analysis of this issue in the Sino-Japanese War of 1894–1895, the Spanish-American War of 1898, and the Russo-Japanese War of 1904–1905. Another topic would be a comparison of American public reaction to the *Virginius* affair in 1873 to that of the sinking of *Maine* in 1898. How and why did the reactions differ? Other topics might involve comparing the value of naval superiority, amphibious landings, or Army-Navy cooperation in American wars between 1846 and 1898.

American historians often overlook Spanish perspectives on the war. Most accounts rely on the Spanish reports translated by the Office of Naval Intelligence. Valuable as this material may be, the documentary sources on the period in Spanish archives located at Segovia, northwest of Madrid, have been ignored by all but a few American historians. Details concerning Spanish naval operations, technological problems, crew training, and strategic decision making would greatly enhance our understanding of the war.

Captain Alfred Thayer Mahan

Select Bibliography of Printed Works

This bibliography on the United States Navy in the Spanish-American War represents a compilation of citations of published sources related to naval topics. The wide variety of subjects included reflect the U.S. Navy's all-encompassing role in the war. Because titles on the diplomacy of the period could make up a bibliography by themselves, the section on diplomatic relations is more selective than other sections. Juvenile literature is not included, but otherwise this bibliography does not distinguish between popular and scholarly works. However, most works published in the first few years after the war are celebratory in nature. Annotations are intended to explain the content of works whose titles are not self-explanatory and to assist the researcher in selecting appropriate works for particular areas of study.

General Works

1. Abbot, Willis John. *Blue Jackets of '98: A History of the Spanish-American War*. New York: Dodd, Mead, 1902. 367 pp.

2. Abrahamson, James L. *America Arms for a New Century: The Making of a Great Military Power*. New York: Free Press, 1981. 253 pp.

   Progressivism in military and naval reform.

3. Alger, Russell Alexander. *The Spanish-American War*. New York: Harper & Bros., 1901. Reprint. Freeport, N.Y.: Books for Libraries Press, 1971. 465 pp.

   Alger was Secretary of the Army during the war. Concentrates on the organization, equipment, and operations of the Army along with the administration of the War Department. Discusses the department's unpreparedness for the war with Spain.

4. Alvarez, José M. *The Spanish-American War: An Annotated Bibliography*. Carlisle Barracks, Pa.: U.S. Army War College, 1991. Various pagings.

5. Armstrong, LeRoy. *Pictorial Atlas Illustrating the Spanish-American War: Comprising a History of the Great Conflict of the United States with Spain.* Chicago: C. F. Beezley, 1898. Reprint. New York: George F. Cram, 1900. 190 pp.

6. Aston, George Grey. *Letters on Amphibious Wars.* London: J. Murray, 1911. 372 pp.

   Two chapters (75 pages) pertain to the Spanish-American War.

7. Axeen, David. "'Heroes of the Engine Room': American Civilization and the War with Spain." *American Quarterly* 36 (1984): 481–502.

   The battleship played a role in contemporary understanding of the Spanish-American War in light of American civilization and values. It represented mechanization and organization, in contrast to individual valor.

8. Barón Fernández, José. *La guerra hispano-norteamericana de 1898.* Sada, A Coruña: Ediciós do Castro, 1993. 273 pp.

9. Bartlett, John Russell. "Watching for the Enemy in the Spanish-American War." *Century Illustrated Monthly* 62 (1901): 907–15.

   An account of the U.S. Navy's Coast Signal Service, of which the author was in charge.

10. Beard, William E. "Adventures of Old Glory." United States Naval Institute *Proceedings* 53 (1927): 318–24.

    Includes a description of events surrounding the raising of the U.S. flag at the surrenders of Santiago and Manila.

11. Beede, Benjamin R., ed. *The War of 1898 and U.S. Interventions, 1898-1934: An Encyclopedia.* New York: Garland, 1994. 751 pp.

12. Blow, Michael. *A Ship to Remember: The Maine and the Spanish-American War.* New York: Morrow, 1992. 496 pp.

    Narrative of the Spanish-American War that includes an extensive discussion of the destruction of *Maine* and the investigations into its cause.

13. Borchers, Duane D., ed. *1898: Efficiency of the Revenue Cutter Service during the Spanish American War.* Annapolis, Md.: Maryland Silver Co., 1994. 80 pp.

This work, Senate Report 1-224, 56th Cong., 1st sess., 1899–1900, includes U.S. Navy and Treasury Department letters written during the war. As a result of the report, revenue cutter officers were placed on an equal footing with officers of the Army and Navy.

14. Borries, Vance von. "The New Empire: America in the Spanish-American War." *Strategy & Tactics* 108 (July–August 1986): 15–24, 41.

15. Bradford, James C., ed. *Crucible of Empire: The Spanish-American War and Its Aftermath*. Annapolis, Md.: Naval Institute Press, 1993. 269 pp.

A collection of scholarly essays on naval and joint topics by noted historians.

16. Bradley, Claudia, et al. *List of Logbooks of U.S. Navy Ships, Stations and Miscellaneous Units, 1801–1947*. Washington, D.C.: National Archives and Records Service, General Services Administration, 1978. 562 pp.

Lists ships by name and the dates covered in available logbooks.

17. Braisted, William Reynolds. *The United States Navy in the Pacific, 1897–1909*. Austin: University of Texas Press, 1958. Reprint. New York: Greenwood Press, 1969. 282 pp.

A study of the U.S. Navy's relationship with American diplomacy in the Far East around the turn of the century, with an examination of the U.S. Navy's interaction with the Germans and insurgents in the Philippines.

18. Bride, Charles. *La guerre hispano-amèricaine de 1898*. Paris: R. Chapelot, 1899. 275 pp.

19. Brooks, Elbridge S. *The Story of Our War with Spain*. Boston: Lothrop, Lee & Shepard, 1899. 349 pp.

20. Buel, James William, ed. *Behind the Guns with American Heroes*. Chicago: International Publishing Co., 1899. 503 pp.

The work consists of chapters by Admiral Dewey and others. Covers both the Spanish-American War and the Philippine Insurrection.

21. Buel, James William. *Leslie's Official History of the Spanish-American War*. Washington, D.C.: Marcus J. Wright, 1899. 614 pp.

Large format, lavishly illustrated.

22. Buel, James William, and Marcus J. Wright. *Our Late Wars: Spain and Our New Possessions*. Washington, D.C.: American Historical Society, 1900. 474 pp.

23. Bujac, [Jean Léopold] Émile. *La guerre hispana-amèricaine*. Paris: H. C. Lavauzelle, [1899]. 420 pp. 2d ed. [1908].

Vol. 4 of the author's *Précis de quelques campaignes contemporaines*.

24. Calvo Poyato, José. *El desastre del 98*. Barcelona, Spain: Plaza & Janés, 1997. 257 pp.

25. Campbell, Alec. "The Spanish-American War." *History Today* 8 (April 1958): 239–47.

Sees a short-lived rise of U.S. expansionism as a major cause of the war.

26. Carmody, Terrence F., and Frederick Merrick Peasley. *United States War Revenue Law of June 13, 1898: With Annotated References to the Rulings on the Same by the Treasury Department from the Passage of the Act to December 22 [i.e. 27] 1898*. Waterbury, Conn.: Dissell Publishing Co., 1899. 613 pp.

27. Cary, R. W. *Naval Operations of the Spanish-American War: Staff Presentation*. Newport, R.I.: Naval War College, 1939. 51 pp.

28. Casau, J., ed. *Homenaje a los héroes de Cavite y de Santiago de Cuba*. Cartegena, Spain: J. Casau, 1923. Unpaged.

Commemorative book on the dedication of a monument in Cartegena, Spain, erected to the memory of Spain's soldiers and sailors who lost their lives in the Battles of Manila Bay and Santiago de Cuba.

29. Central Bureau of Engraving, New York. *Our Heroes of the Spanish-American War*. New York: Central Bureau of Engraving, 1898.

Portraits of fifteen notable U.S. Army and Navy officers.

30. Chadwick, French Ensor. *The Relations of the United States and Spain: The Spanish-American War.* 2 vols. New York: Scribner's, 1911. Reprint. New York: Russell & Russell, 1968.

Emphasis is placed on naval operations. The work includes extensive quotations from wartime documents as well as appendices listing ships in commission during the war, vessels purchased, and vessels converted. Other appendices list ships that entered Cuban ports and casualties to American forces.

31. Chidsey, Donald Barr. *The Spanish-American War: A Behind-the-Scenes Account of the War in Cuba.* New York: Crown Publishers, 1971. 191 pp.

Covers the war at Manila and Puerto Rico, as well.

32. *Chronology of the War with Spain.* Washington, D.C.: N.p., 1899. 4 pp.

Daniel Murray Pamphlet Collection (Library of Congress). Covers period 25 January to 12 August 1898.

33. Clarke, G. S. "Naval Aspects of the Spanish-American War." Chapter 5, pp. 123–74, in *The Naval Annual, 1899.* Edited by T. A. Brassey. Portsmouth, Great Britain: J. Griffin, 1899.

An analytical account of naval events of the war with an eye toward operational and tactical lessons.

34. Cooling, Benjamin Franklin. *Gray Steel and Blue Water Navy: The Formative Years of America's Military-Industrial Complex, 1881–1917.* Hamden, Conn.: Archon Books, 1979. 286 pp.

Argues that the New Navy's need for steel armor and ordnance forged the military-industrial bonds that mutually benefited U.S. industry and national defense.

35. Cosmas, Graham A. *An Army for Empire: The United States Army and the Spanish-American War.* Columbia: University of Missouri Press, 1971. 334 pp. Reprints. Shippensburg, Pa.: White Mane, 1994. 349 pp. College Station: Texas A&M University Press, 1998. 368 pp.

View of the U.S. Army in the war against Spain from the perspective of the civilian and uniformed leadership in the War

Department. Cosmas argues that the Army's wartime misfortunes had less to do with fundamental mistakes in the War Department than from hurried attempts to implement its policies with a shortage of trained personnel and inadequate supplies. The reprinted editions include an introduction reviewing the historiography of the U.S. Army during the period as well as additional material on the African-American experience and the Battles of San Juan Hill and El Caney. Also included is a discussion of the Army's postwar role in occupying Cuba and the Philippines.

36. Cram, George Franklin. *Cram's Big War Atlas: Showing All Fighting Territory.* New York: George Cram, [1898]. 22 pp. Also published by Chicago: E. A. Weeks Co., 1898.

37. Cugle, Frances. *A Brief History of the Spanish-American War.* Harrisburg, Pa.: Kurzenknabe Press, 1898. 91 pp.

   Includes text of President McKinley's Cuban message to Congress on 11 April 1898 and a chronology of important events.

38. Davis, George Theron. *A Navy Second to None: The Development of Modern American Naval Policy.* New York: Harcourt, Brace, 1940. Reprint. Westport, Conn.: Greenwood Press, 1971. 508 pp.

39. Díez Alegría, Manuel. "La esplendida guerrita de los Americanos," *Revue Internationale d'Histoire Militaire* 56 (1984): 9–47.

40. Dutton, Charles J. "American Prison Camp." *Commonweal* 33 (3 January 1941): 270–72.

   Account of the prisoner of war camp established at Portsmouth Navy Yard in Kittery, Maine, for the Spanish sailors captured with Cervera's fleet.

41. Dyal, Donald H. *Historical Dictionary of the Spanish American War.* Westport, Conn.: Greenwood Press, 1996. 378 pp.

42. Evans, Stephen H. *The United States Coast Guard, 1790–1915: A Definitive History.* Annapolis, Md.: Naval Institute Press, 1949. 228 pp.

Chapter 12, "Of War and Peace," focuses on the revenue cutters incorporated into the Navy's fleets at Manila and in Cuban waters.

43. Fernández Almagro, Melchor. *Historia política de la España contemporánea*. 3 vols. Madrid: Alianza Editorial, 1968.

Vol. 3, *1898–1902*, provides an account of the war from the point of view of Spanish political history.

44. Figuero, Javier. *La España del desastre*. Barcelona, Spain: Plaza & Janés, 1997. 372 pp.

45. Freidel, Frank. *The Splendid Little War*. Boston: Little, Brown, 1958. 314 pp.

An illustrated narrative that focuses on the major U.S. Army and Navy actions in the campaigns for Manila, Cuba, and Puerto Rico.

46. Gauvreau, Charles F. *Reminiscences of the Spanish-American War in Cuba and the Philippines*. St. Albans, Vt.: Messenger Office, Printers, 1912. 141 pp. Reprint. Rouses Point, N.Y.: The Authors Publishing Co., 1915. 160 pp.

Gauvreau was a private in the 21st Infantry Regiment. His account includes descriptions of conditions on board a transport and the landing in Cuba.

47. Giddings, Howard A. *Exploits of the Signal Corps in the War with Spain*. Kansas City, Mo., 1900. 126 pp.

Includes a discussion of the Signal Corps' role in locating Cervera's squadron, and in directing naval gunfire during the bombardment of Santiago de Cuba.

48. Goldstein, Donald M., et al. *The Spanish-American War: The Story and Photographs*. Washington, D.C.: Brassey's, 1998. 192 pp.

49. Gómez Núñez, Severo. *La guerra hispano-americana: Puerto-Rico y Filipinas*. Madrid: Ipr. Del Cuerpo de Artillería, 1902. 254 pp.

50. Green, Nathan C. *The War with Spain and Story of Spain and Cuba*. Baltimore, Md.: International News & Book Co., 1898. 532 pp.

This work is mostly a series of articles on subjects related to the Cuban Insurrection and the Spanish-American War. Includes information on the commerce of the Spanish colonies.

51. Hagan, Kenneth J. *This People's Navy: The Making of American Sea Power.* New York: Free Press, 1991. 434 pp.

52. Halstead, Murat. *Full Official History of the War with Spain.* Chicago: C. F. Breezley; Dominion Co.; Philadelphia: J. H. Moore, 1899. 794 pp.

53. *Harper's Pictorial History of the War with Spain.* New York: Harper & Bros., 1899. 507 pp.

    Also published in two volumes.

54. Harris, Brayton. *The Age of the Battleship, 1890–1922.* New York: Franklin Watts, 1965. 212 pp.

55. Hart, Kevin R. "Towards A Citizen Sailor: The History of the Naval Militia Movement, 1888–1898." *American Neptune* 33 (1973): 258–79.

    Discusses the history of the Naval Militia and the country's attempts to develop a naval reserve that could augment the Navy's strength in wartime.

56. *Hero Tales of the American Soldier and Sailor As Told by the Heroes Themselves and Their Comrades.* Philadelphia: Century Manufacturing Co.; New York: W. W. Wilson, 1899. 503 pp.

    Includes firsthand accounts by both enlisted and officers in the U.S. Army and Navy.

57. Herrick, Walter R., Jr. *The American Naval Revolution.* Baton Rouge: Louisiana State University Press, 1966. 274 pp.

    This study examines a revolution in doctrine that transformed the U.S. Navy from a coastal defense fleet to a unified battle fleet capable of offensive action.

58. *Historical Sketch of the Naval and Military Order of the Spanish-American War.* St. Petersburg, Fla.: National Headquarters Office, 1958. 55 pp.

59. Hollis, Ira Nelson. "The Navy in the War with Spain." *Atlantic Monthly* 82 (1898–1899), 605–16.

60. ____. "The Uncertain Factors in Naval Conflict." *Atlantic Monthly* 81 (1898), 728–36.

61. *Illustrated War News*. New York: [F. Tousey], 1898.

    Monthly publication. Vol. 1, no. 1–4 (May–August).

62. Johnston, Edgar. *The Great American-Spanish War Scenes with Official Photographs by United States Naval Photographer, E. H. Hart. A History of the War in Cuba and the United States Conflict with Spain.* Chicago: W. B. Conkey, 1898. 227 pp.

63. Johnston, William A. *History Up To Date: A Concise Account of the War of 1898 between the United States and Spain, Its Causes and the Treaty of Paris*. New York: A. S. Barnes, 1899. 258 pp.

64. Jornadas de Historia Maritima (6th, 1990: Madrid, Spain). *La marina ante el 98. (II): genesis y desarrollo de un conflicto.* Madrid: Instituto de Historia y Cultural Naval, 1990. 167 pp.

    Four of these nine papers delivered at a cycle of conferences held in November 1990 concern naval aspects: "De Cavite a Santiago," by José Blanco Núñez; "Lo naval en el noventa y ocho," by Eliseo Alvarez Arenas; "La guerra olvidada de Puerto Rico," by José Cervera Pery; and "La armada en el debate político de la postguerra," by Fernando De Bordje.

65. Keenan, Henry F. *The Conflict with Spain: A History of the War Based upon Official Reports and Descriptions of Eyewitnesses.* Philadelphia: P. W. Ziegler, 1898. 601 pp.

    Includes forty-five pages of reports by naval officers. The work is heavily illustrated with sketches and photographs.

66. Keller, Allan. *The Spanish-American War: A Compact History.* New York: Hawthorn Books, 1969. 258 pp.

    No footnotes. Bibliography contains only published sources.

67. King, William Nephew. *The Story of the Spanish-American War, and the Revolt in the Philippines.* New York: N.p., 1898. Reprint. New York: P. F. Collier, 1900. 272 pp.

    Large format, lavishly illustrated.

68. Kiralfy, Imre. *Our Naval Victories: An American Naval Spectacle.* N.p.: Strauss, 1898. 29 pp.

69. Leech, Margaret. *In the Days of McKinley.* New York: Harper & Row, 1959. Reprints. Westport, Conn.: Greenwood Press, 1975. Norwalk, Conn.: Easton Press, 1986. 686 pp.

70. Leuchtenberg, William E. "The Needless War with Spain." *American Heritage* 8 (1957): 32–41, 95. Also in *Times of Trial*, edited by Allan Nevins, 177–96. New York: Alfred A. Knopf, 1958.

71. Lodge, Henry Cabot. *The War with Spain.* New York: Harper & Bros., 1899. Reprint. New York: Arno Press and the New York Times, 1970. 276 pp.

    Contains eighty-three illustrations. The appendices include select diplomatic documents, including the text of the Treaty of Paris.

72. Long, John Davis. *The New American Navy.* 2 vols. New York: Outlook, 1903. Reprint. New York: Arno Press, 1979. 555 pp. [in one volume].

    Illustrated with drawings by Henry Reuterdahl. Long was Secretary of the Navy under Presidents William McKinley and Theodore Roosevelt. Vol. 1 discusses the birth, building, organization, and administration of the New Steel Navy, as well as early naval operations of the Spanish-American War. Vol. 2 discusses the remaining operations of the Spanish-American War as well as subsequent events in the Philippines, Samoa, and China. The appendix includes documents related to the Sampson-Schley controversy.

73. Louisiana State Museum, New Orleans. *The Spanish-American War of 1898, Liberty for Cuba and World Power for the United States.* Edited by James J. A. Fortier. New Orleans: Louisiana State Museum, 1939.

    A description of the participation of men and units from Louisiana including the 1st Naval Battalion of Louisiana.

74. Luce, Stephen B. "The Spanish-American War." *North American Review* 194 (1911): 612–27.

    An essay review of French Ensor Chadwick, *The Relations of the United States and Spain,* entry no. 30.

75. McGarvey, Paul Brian. "The Development of the Modern United States Navy and the War with Spain, 1880-1898." Master's thesis, East Stroudsburg University, 1987. 114 pp.

76. Maclay, Edgar Stanton. *A History of the United States Navy From 1775-1901*. 3 vols. New York: D. Appleton, 1901.

   Vol. 3, pp. 39–433, treats the Spanish-American War. Appendices include a "Roll of Honor in the War with Spain."

77. [McNally, Bernard, comp.] *Soldiers and Sailors of New Jersey in the Spanish-American War: Embracing a Chronological Account of the Army and Navy*. Newark, N.J.: B. McNally, 1898. 46 pp.

   Includes information on the Naval Reserve of New Jersey, the training ship USS *Portsmouth,* and U.S. auxiliary cruiser *Badger* with its rough log and list of officers.

78. Marshall, Samuel L. A. *The War to Free Cuba: The Military History of the Spanish-American War*. New York: Franklin Watts, 1966. 79 pp.

79. Mason, Gregory. *Remember the Maine*. New York: Henry Holt, 1939. 312 pp.

   A popular narrative of the entire war.

80. Matthews, Franklin. *Our Navy in Time of War (1861–1898)*. New York: D. Appleton, 1899. 275 pp.

   Intended for students and includes one chapter each on the Battles of Manila Bay and Santiago de Cuba.

81. Medel, José Antonio. *The Spanish-American War and Its Results*. Havana, Cuba: P. Fernandez, 1932. 122 pp.

   A general history of the war. Medel was a cavalry captain in the Cuban army.

82. Miles, Nelson A. "The War with Spain." *North American Review* 168 (May, June 1899): 513–29, 749–60; 169 (July 1899): 125–37.

83. Millis, Walter. *The Martial Spirit: A Study of Our War with Spain*. Boston: Houghton Mifflin; New York: Literary Guild of America, 1931. Reprints. New York: Arno Press, 1979. Chicago: I. R. Dee, 1989. 427 pp.

   A general narrative of the war from a satirical perspective.

84. Minton, Telfair Marriott. *History of the First Battalion Naval Militia, New York, 1891–1911.* New York: Knickerbocker Press (G. P. Putnam's Sons), 1911. 188 pp.

    During the Spanish-American War members of the battalion served on board USS *Yankee* in the Cuban theater and on board USS *Nahant* in New York Harbor.

85. Mitchell, D. W. *History of the Modern American Navy: From 1883 through Pearl Harbor.* New York: Alfred A. Knopf, 1946. 475 pp.

    Contains three chapters on the Spanish-American War, treating the beginnings, Pacific operations, and Atlantic operations.

86. Morris, Charles. *The War with Spain: A Complete History of the War of 1898 between the United States and Spain.* Philadelphia: J. B. Lippincott, 1899. 383 pp.

87. Musicant, Ivan. *The Banana Wars: A History of United States Military Intervention in Latin America from the Spanish-American War to the Invasion of Panama.* New York: Macmillan, 1990. 470 pp.

88. _____. *Empire by Default: The Spanish-American War and the Dawn of the American Century.* New York: Henry Holt, 1998. 750 pp.

    A military and naval account of the war with significant attention to diplomacy.

89. Musick, John R. *Lights and Shadows of Our War with Spain.* New York: J. S. Oglivie, 1898. 224 pp.

90. *Naval Actions and History, 1799–1898.* Boston: Military History Society of Massachusetts, 1902. 398 pp.

    Asa Walker, Captain, USN, "The Battle of Manila Bay," pp. 365–86, recounts his experiences as a participant in command of USS *Concord.*

91. "Naval Militia in Service." *Harper's Weekly* 42 (30 April 1898): 417–18.

    Emergency manning of old monitors with New York Naval Militia.

92. New York (State) Naval Militia. *Report of the Captain of the Naval Militia of New York to the Adjutant-General on the War with Spain.* New York: Wynkoop Hallenbeck Crawford, 1898. 72 pp.

The author was Captain J. W. Miller.

93. Nofi, Albert A. *The Spanish-American War, 1898.* Conshohocken, Pa.: Combined Books, 1997. 352 pp.

Each chapter contains several sidebars of brief biographies, orders of battle, and discussions of special topics.

94. Otis, James. *The Boys of '98.* Boston: Dana Estes, 1898. 386 pp.

This is an operational narrative of the war that sometimes turns into a strict chronology.

95. O'Toole, George J. A. *The Spanish War: An American Epic—1898.* New York: Norton, 1984. 447 pp.

General popular history of the war. The author emphasizes America's transition to empire.

96. *Our War with Spain: The Army and Navy, Cuba, Puerto Rico, Hawaii and the Philippines.* Chicago: N.p., 1898.

Large-format book of photographs.

97. Parkerson, A. C. *How Uncle Sam Fights: Or, Modern Warfare, How Conducted.* Baltimore, Md.: R. H. Woodward, 1898. 464 pp.

98. Paullin, Charles Oscar. *Paullin's History of Naval Administration, 1775–1911.* Annapolis, Md.: U.S. Naval Institute, 1968. 485 pp.

A collection of articles from the United States Naval Institute *Proceedings.*

99. Payne, Stanley G. *Politics and the Military in Modern Spain.* Stanford, Calif.: Stanford University Press, 1967. 574 pp.

Treats the years 1808 to 1966. See particularly chapters 5 and 6, "The Colonial Disaster" and "The Aftermath."

100. Pearson Publishing Company. *Photographic History of the Spanish-American War: A Pictorial and Descriptive Record of Events on Land and Sea with Portraits and Biographies of Leaders on Both Sides.* New York: Pearson Publishing Co., 1898. 136 pp.

Also published as *Pearson's Official War History: A Complete Pictorial History of the Spanish-American Struggle of 1898.*

101. Peuser, Richard W. "Documenting United States Naval Activities During the Spanish-American War." *Prologue: The Journal of the National Archives* 30 (1998): 33–45.

Describes the holdings at the National Archives that document U.S. naval activities during the period.

102. *Photographic History of the War with Spain.* Baltimore, Md.: R. H. Woodward, 1898. 88 pp.

Also covers the U.S. Navy, Spain, Cuba, Puerto Rico, Hawaii, and the Philippines.

103. *Pictorial Souvenir of the Spanish-American War, Army and Navy.* New York: United Publishers of America, 1899. 16 pp.

104. Plüddemann, Max. *Comments of Rear-Admiral Plüddemann, German Navy, on Main Features of the Spanish-American War* (Translated from the German). Washington, D.C.: Government Printing Office, 1898. 18 pp. Reprint. "Main Features of the Spanish-American War." *Journal of the Royal United Service Institution* 43 (1899): 654–66.

Reprinted with seven other essays by the U.S. Navy Department, Office of Naval Intelligence as War Note No. 2 in *Information from Abroad* (Washington, D.C.: Government Printing Office, 1898–1899). The essay includes technical comments on battles, naval gunnery, coaling, and the operations of naval auxiliaries.

105. Potter, E. B., et al. eds. *Sea Power: A Naval History.* 2d ed. Annapolis, Md.: Naval Institute Press, 1981. 419 pp.

See chapter 17, "The Spanish-American War." Intended "for general reading, as a reference work and as a textbook."

106. Rice, Wallace. *Heroic Deeds in Our War with Spain: An Episodic History of the Fighting of 1898 on Sea and Shore.* Chicago: George M. Hill, [1898]. 447 pp.

107. Richards, Julian W. *A Handbook of the Spanish-American War of 1898 and the Insurrection in the Philippines.* N.p.: Republican Printing Co., 1899. 36 pp.

Includes a chronological record of battles, messages of President McKinley, and operations of the Army and Navy.

108. Rodríguez González, Agustín Ramón. *La guerra del 98: Las campañas de Cuba, Puerto Rico y Filipinas.* Madrid, Spain: Agualarga Editores, S. L., 1998. 165 pp.

A lavishly illustrated, popular narrative of the war.

109. Russell, Henry B. *An Illustrated History of Our War with Spain: Its Causes, Incidents and Results.* Hartford, Conn.: A. D. Worthington, 1898. 796 pp.

Two thirds of this book is devoted to prewar events such as the Ten-Years War, political trouble in Spain, and diplomacy.

110. *Saginaw: Her Soldiers and Sailors in the Spanish-American War, 1898.* [Saginaw, Mich.]: Goodbody & Stilwell, [1899]. Unpaged.

111. Shewey, Arista C. *Shewey's Atlas of the Spanish-American War.* Chicago: N.p., 1898. 23 pp.

112. Sigsbee, Charles D., et al. *The United States Navy in the Spanish-American War of 1898: Narratives of the Chief Events.* 2 vols. N.p., 1899.

This work is a collection of magazine articles published together. Vol. 1 contains narratives of U.S. naval officers, and vol. 2 contains narratives of other naval officers.

113. Smith, Joseph. *The Spanish-American War: Conflict in the Caribbean and the Pacific, 1895–1902.* London: Longman, 1994. 262 pp.

114. Spain. Ministerio de Marina. *Correspondencia oficial, referente á las operationes navales durante la guerra con los Estados Unidos.* Madrid: Imprenta del Ministerio de Marina, 1899. 310 pp.

115. *The Spanish-American War, the Events of the War Described by Eye Witnesses.* New York: Herbert S. Stone, 1899. 228 pp.

Accounts of events by newspaper correspondents.

116. *The Spanish War Journal.* Washington, D.C.: [L. C. Dyer, 1901–07].

The official organ of the Spanish war veterans.

117. Spears, John Randolph. *The History of Our Navy: From Its Origins to the End of the War with Spain, 1775–1898.* 5 vols. N.Y.: Charles Scribner's Sons, 1897–1899. Vol. 5, *Our Navy in the War with Spain.* 406 pp.

Another edition of vol. 5, published in 1899, is 554 pp. and contains a fuller discussion of the U.S. Navy between the American Civil War and the war with Spain.

118. Spector, Ronald H. *Professors of War: The Naval War College and the Development of the Naval Profession.* Newport, R.I.: Naval War College Press, 1977. 185 pp.

Studies the role of the Naval War College in the professionalization of the U.S. Navy from 1884 to 1917. Chapter 7 includes a summary of the war plans against Spain developed by the War College, the Office of Naval Intelligence, and special boards convened by the Secretary of the Navy.

119. _____. "The Triumph of Professional Ideology: The U.S. Navy in the 1890s." In *In Peace and War: Interpretations of American Naval History, 1775–1984,* 2d ed., edited by Kenneth J. Hagan, 174–85. Westport, Conn.: Greenwood Press, 1984. 395 pp. 1st edition, 1978.

How sea control and the ideas of Mahan came to dominate American naval policy.

120. Sprout, Harold, and Margaret Sprout. *The Rise of American Naval Power, 1776–1918.* Princeton, N.J.: Princeton University Press, 1946. Reprint. Annapolis, Md.: Naval Institute Press, 1990. 448 pp.

121. Strait, Newton Allen. *Alphabetical List of Battles, 1754–1900.* Washington, D.C.: N.p., 1905. Reprint. Detroit: Gale Research Co., 1968. 252 pp.

Includes a "Summary of Events of the Spanish-American War."

122. Street, Arthur Irwin. *A Chronicle of the War: Including Historical Documents, Army and Navy Movements, Roster of State Troops, etc.* N.p., 1898. 160 pp.

123. Sweetman, Jack. *American Naval History: An Illustrated Chronology of the U.S. Navy and Marine Corps, 1775–Present.* 2d ed. Annapolis, Md.: Naval Institute Press, 1991. 376 pp.

124. Tanham, George J. "Service Relations Sixty Years Ago." *Military Affairs* 23 (1959): 139–48.

125. Tavares, Raul. *De Cavite a Santiago de Cuba (guerra hispano-americana)*. Genova: Stab. tip. P. Pellas, 1902. 148 pp.

An account of the war, in Portuguese, from the point of view of a Brazilian navy lieutenant.

126. Titherington, Richard Hanfield. *A History of the Spanish-American War of 1898*. New York: D. Appleton, 1900. Reprint. Freeport, N.Y.: Books for Libraries Press, 1971. 415 pp.

127. Trask, David F. *The War with Spain in 1898*. New York: Macmillan, 1981. Reprint, Lincoln: University of Nebraska Press, 1996. 654 pp.

The standard scholarly study of the Spanish-American War that includes extensive coverage of naval issues and activity.

128. Traverso, Edmund. *The Spanish-American War: A Study in Policy Change*. Lexington, Mass.: D. C. Heath, 1968. 140 pp.

129. *Uncle Sam's Navy*. Philadelphia: Historical Pub. Co., 1898. A single volume in twelve separate parts.

Large-format book of photographs.

130. U.S. Congress. House Committee on Pensions. *Spanish-American War Pensions. Hearings before the Committee on Pensions on H.R.2*. 66th Cong. 1st sess., 1919. 22 pp.

131. U.S. Congress. House. *Spanish-American War Pension Act of May 1, 1926*. 69th Cong. 1st sess., 1926. H. Doc. 376. 2 pp.

132. U.S. Navy Department. *Annual Reports of the Navy Department for the Year 1898*. Washington, D.C.: Government Printing Office, 1898. 930 pp.

This publication contains a wealth of administrative and financial information on the Navy Department in the reports of the eight bureaus and the Commandant of the Marine Corps. The report from the Bureau of Steam Engineering contains twenty-two diagrams of engineering plants in U.S. Navy warships.

133. _____. *Appendix to the Report of the Chief of the Bureau of Navigation, 1898*. Washington, D.C.: Government Printing Office, 1898. 740 pp.

This publication is a collection of documents related to U.S. naval operations during the war with Spain. It includes photographs and diagrams of battle damage to Spanish vessels as well as charts of areas of operations.

134. U.S. Treasury Department. Revenue Cutter Service. *The United States Revenue Cutter Service in the War with Spain, 1898*. Washington, D.C.: Government Printing Office, 1899. 49 pp.

135. U.S. War Department. Adjutant General's Office. *Correspondence Relating to the War with Spain and Conditions Growing Out of the Same: Including the Insurrection in the Philippine Islands and the China Relief Expedition, April 15, 1898 to July 30, 1902*. 2 vols. Washington, D.C.: Government Printing Office, 1902. Reprint. Washington, D.C.: Center for Military History, 1993. 1489 pp.

Vol. 2 includes a 130-page index. Documents include a wealth of material on joint operations.

136. *U.S. Navy Album*. N.p.: Koerner & Hayes, 1898. 16 pp.

137. Venzon, Anne Cipriano. *The Spanish-American War: An Annotated Bibliography*. New York: Garland Publishing, 1990. 255 pp.

A selective bibliography that includes the majority of scholarly works written in English between 1898 and 1986. The 1,180 entries include topics such as music and fiction as well as books and articles on the Philippine-American War, 1899–1902.

138. Watterson, Henry. *History of the Spanish-American War: Embracing a Complete Review of Our Relations with Spain*. New York: Werner, 1898. 474 pp.

139. Webb, William Joe. "The Spanish-American War and United States Army Shipping." *American Neptune* 40 (July 1980): 167–91.

Problems and solutions of the Army's Quartermaster Department in its efforts to ship U.S. Army personnel to Cuba, Puerto Rico, and the Philippines.

140. Weigley, Russell F. *The American Way of War: A History of United States Military Strategy and Policy*. New York: Macmillan, 1973. Reprint. Bloomington: Indiana University Press, 1977. 584 pp.

See in particular 9, "A Strategy of Sea Power and Empire: Stephen B. Luce and Alfred Thayer Mahan."

141. Werstein, Irving. *1898: The Spanish-American War Told with Pictures*. New York: Cooper Square, 1966. 128 pp.

142. _____. *Turning Point for America: The Story of the Spanish-American War*. New York: Julian Messner, 1964. 191 pp.

143. White, Trumbull. *Our War with Spain for Cuba's Freedom: Including a Description and History of Cuba, Spain, Philippine Island: Or, Army and Navy, Fighting Strength, Coast Defenses, and Our Relations with Other Nations, etc.* Chicago: Monarch Book Co., 1898. 416 pp.

144. _____. *Pictorial History of Our War with Spain for Cuba's Freedom . . .* Chicago: Freedom Publishing Co., 1898. Also published under the title *Our War with Spain for Cuba's Freedom*. 578 pp.

Includes a chapter of short personal reminiscences of participants and journalists.

145. Wilcox, Marrion, ed. *A Short History of the War with Spain*. New York: Frederick A. Stokes, 1898. 350 pp.

146. Wilkie, John E., ed. *The American-Spanish War: A History by the War Leaders*. Norwich, Conn.: Charles C. Haskell & Son, 1899. 607 pp.

Chapters cover a wide range of topics written by the war's participants. In addition to operational accounts, topics include women's work in the war, the Secret Service, war legislation, and financial administration.

147. Wilson, Herbert Wrigley. *Battleships in Action*. 2 vols. Boston: Little, Brown, 1926. Reprints. Grosse Point, Mich.: Scholarly Press, 1969. Annapolis, Md.: Naval Institute Press, 1995.

Vol. 1, chapters 7 and 8 cover the Spanish-American War.

148. _____. *The Downfall of Spain: Naval History of the Spanish-American War*. London: Low, Marston & Co., 1900. Reprint. New York: B. Franklin, 1971. 451 pp.

An account of the destruction of USS *Maine* and naval operations during the war. The book includes more technical details of the fighting vessels than usually appear in an operational study.

149. *With Our Soldiers and Sailors, Afloat and Ashore*. New York: Riley Bros., 1898. 39 pp.

150. Wright, Marcus J. *Official History of the Spanish-American War . . .* Washington, D.C.: N.p., [1900]. 617 pp.

An illustrated narrative of the war that provides information on the climate, production, history, and people of Cuba, Puerto Rico, the Philippines, and Hawaii.

151. Young, James Rankin. *Reminiscences and Thrilling Stories by Returned Heroes*. Washington, D.C.: R. A. Dinsmore, 1898. Reprint. Chicago: Monroe Book Co., 1899. 664 pp.

Includes chapters on hospital work, nurses, and poetry of the war.

152. Ziel, Ron. *Birth of the American Century: Centennial History of the Spanish-American War*. Edited by Jedidiah Clauss. Mattituck, N.Y.: Amereon House, 1997. 304 pp.

A heavily illustrated history of the war.

Background and Preparation

Cuban Insurrection and Relations with Spain

153. Akers, Charles E. "The Situation in Cuba." *Harper's Weekly* 42 (12 March 1898): 261.

154. *Antes del "desastre": Orígenes y antecedentes de la crisis del 98.* Madrid: Universidad Complutense de Madrid, Departmento de Historia Contemporánea, 1996. 480 pp.

155. Beck, Henry Houghton. *Cuba's Fight for Freedom, and the War with Spain: A Comprehensive, Accurate and Thrilling History of the Spanish Kingdom and Its Latest and Fairest Colony* . . . Philadelphia: Globe Bible Publishing Co., 1898. 569 pp.

156. Benjamin, Jules R. *The United States and the Origins of the Cuban Revolution: An Empire of Liberty in an Age of National Liberation.* Princeton, N.J.: Princeton University Press, 1990. 235 pp.

    United States–Cuban relations, from the Ten-Years' War to the Communist Revolution.

157. Castañeda, Tiburcio P. *La explosión del Maine y la guerra de los Estados Unidos con España*. Havana, Cuba: Librería e imprenta "La moderna poesía," 1925. 333 pp.

Primarily a diplomatic history of the war, with emphasis on U.S. ulterior motives in declaring war and the causes of the explosion of *Maine*. The author quotes extensively from contemporary documents.

158. Chapman, Charles Edward. *A History of the Cuban Republic: A Study in Hispanic American Politics*. New York: Macmillan, 1927. Reprints. New York: Octagon Books, 1969. Westport, Conn.: Greenwood Press, 1971. 685 pp.

159. Companys Monclús, Julián. *España en 1898: Entre la diplomacia y la guerra*. Madrid: Ministerio de Asuntos Exteriores, 1991. 374 pp.

Focuses on the diplomatic negotiations concerning Cuba between Spain and McKinley's administration, concluding with the rupture of diplomatic relations. Chapter 8 discusses the destruction of *Maine*.

160. Cortada, James W. *Two Nations over Time: Spain and the United States, 1776–1977*. Westport, Conn.: Greenwood Press, 1978. 305 pp.

See chapter 7, "The Spanish-American War."

161. Flack, Horace Edgar. *Spanish American Diplomatic Relations Preceeding the War of 1898*. Baltimore, Md.: Johns Hopkins Press, 1906. 95 pp.

Topics cover belligerency or insurgency, the legal case for intervention, and Spain's efforts to avoid war with the United States.

162. Healy, David F. *The United States in Cuba, 1898–1902: Generals, Politicians and the Search for Policy*. Madison: University of Wisconsin Press, 1963. 260 pp.

163. Kelly, David E. "Prelude to the Spanish-American War: The Cuban Junta, the deLome Letter, the Sinking of the *Maine*." *Marine Corps Gazette* 82 (February 1998): 64–69.

First in a series of articles about the war that discusses the new roles that the Marines began to take on.

164. Langley, Lester D. *The Cuban Policy of the United States: A Brief History.* New York: John Wiley & Sons, [1968]. 203 pp.

165. Lee, Fitzhugh, and Joseph Wheeler. *Cuba's Struggle against Spain with the Causes for American Intervention and a Full Account of the Spanish-American War: Including Final Peace Negotiations.* New York: American Historical Press, 1899. 676 pp.

   Includes chapters entitled "A Story of Santiago," by Theodore Roosevelt, and "A Description of the Destruction of the 'Maine'," by Richard Wainwright.

166. Miller, Richard Hayes, ed. *American Imperialism in 1898: The Quest for National Fulfillment.* New York: Wiley, 1970. 206 pp.

167. Offner, John L. "President McKinley and the Origins of the Spanish-American War." Ph.D. diss., Pennsylvania State University, 1957. 401 pp.

168. _____. *An Unwanted War: The Diplomacy of the United States and Spain over Cuba, 1895–1898.* Chapel Hill: University of North Carolina Press, 1992. 306 pp.

169. Rubens, Horatio Seymour. *Liberty: The Story of Cuba.* New York: Brewer, Warren & Putnam, 1932. Reprint. New York: AMS Press, 1970. 447 pp.

170. *Spanish Diplomatic Correspondence and Documents, 1896–1900: Presented to the Cortes by the Minister of State.* Translation. Washington, D.C.: Government Printing Office, 1905. 398 pp.

171. Thomas, Hugh. *Cuba: The Pursuit of Freedom.* New York: Harper & Row, 1971. Rev. ed. New York: Da Capo Press, 1998. 1,696 pp.

   A history of Cuba from 1762 to the 1960s.

172. U.S. Congress. Senate. *Consular Correspondence Respecting the Condition of the Reconcentrados in Cuba, the State of the War in That Island, and the Prospects of the Projected Autonomy.* 55th Cong., 2d sess. 1898. S. Doc. 230 (Serial 3610). 91 pp.

173. Volckmer, Otto. *Historical Sketch from the Destruction of the Maine to the Battle of Manila: A Short History in Memory of the Lost Heroes of the Maine.* New York: M. F. Tobin, 1898. 29 pp.

USS **Maine**

174. Allen, Thomas B. ed. "What Really Sank the *Maine*?" *Naval History* 11 (March/April 1998): 30–39.

Summary of a report by Advanced Marine Enterprises that used computer modeling to examine the possible causes of *Maine*'s destruction. Report concludes that a mine was the most likely cause.

175. Basoco, Richard M. "What Really Happened to the Maine?" *American History Illustrated* 1 (June 1966): 12–22.

Reviews the known facts and the speculations but arrives at no conclusion.

176. Beehler, W. H. "Experiences of a Naval Attache." *Century Illustrated Monthly* 76 (1908): 946–55.

Author provides a detailed discussion on how a mine could have destroyed *Maine*.

177. Bronin, Andrew, comp. *Remember the Maine!* Edited by Cris Johnson. New York: Grossman Publishers, 1973.

A portfolio of fifteen pieces: one introductory pamphlet, nine facsimiles of contemporary documents, and five explanatory broadsheets.

178. Buettell, Roger B. "Remember the 'Maine!'" *Down East* (March 1966): 26–29, 54–55.

179. Butler, Charles Henry. *The Responsibility of Spain for the Destruction of the United States Battleship Maine in Havana Harbor, February 15, 1898*. New York: Evening Post Job Printing House, 1902. 91 pp.

180. Calleja Leal, Guillermo G. "La voladura del Maine." *Revista de Historia Militar* 34 (1990): 163–96.

   Proposes possibility that rebel Cubans residing in the United States, with ties to Garibaldi anarchists also living in the United States, were responsible for the destruction of *Maine*.

181. *La catástrofe del Maine: relación circunstanciada de la terrible explosión ocurrida á bordo del acorazado norte-americano "Maine" en la noche del 15 Febrero de 1898*. Havana, Cuba: "El Figaro," 1898. 24 pp.

182. Chidwick, John P. *"Remember the Maine!" An Historical Narrative of the Battleship Maine as Told by Its Chaplain, the Right Reverened [sic] Monsignor John P. Chidwick, by Harry T. Cook . . .* Winchester, Va: Winchester Printers and Stationers, [1935]. 34 pp.

183. Cluverius, W. T. "A Midshipman on the *Maine*." United States Naval Institute *Proceedings* 44 (1918): 236–48.

   Cluverius was on board *Maine* the night she was destroyed. The article is an account of the ship's last days.

184. Companys Monclús, Julián. *De la explosión del Maine a la ruptura de relaciones diplomáticas entre Estados Unidos y España*. Barcelona, Spain: Departament de Geografia i Història, Facultat de Lletres de l'Estudi General de Lleida, Universitat de Barcelona, 1989. 147 pp.

185. Duncan, John E. "Remember the *Maine*, One More Time." *Naval History* 4 (Spring 1990): 58–62.

   An account of the raising of the wreck, 1910–1912.

186. "Foreign Expert Opinion on the Maine Disaster." *Scientific American* 106 (1898): 322–23.

The "English technical press" supported the findings of the U.S. naval court of inquiry that the destruction of *Maine* was premeditated and caused from the outside.

187. Greig, Julius. *The Immediate Cause of the War with Spain: From the Personal Narrative of J. Greig . . . [concerning] the Plot Which Resulted in the Total Destruction of the United States Battleship "Maine" . . . as Dictated to C. H. McLellan*. Boston: Charles H. McLellan, 1899. 51 pp.

188. [Hambright, Tom]. *Battleship Maine Plot: Key West Cemetery*. Key West, Fla.: Tom Hambright, 1990. 47 pp.

189. Hammersmith, Jack L. "Raising the Battleship *Maine*." *Industrial Archaeology* 15 (1980): 318–29.

Sees the thorough documentation of the *Maine* wreck before its re-sinking at sea in 1912 as "a model for preservationists and industrial archaeologists."

190. Hansen, Ib S., and Dana M. Wegner. "Centenary of the Destruction of USS *Maine*: A Technical Historical Review." *Naval Engineers Journal* 110 (March 1998): 93–104.

Reviews the technical investigations from 1898 to the present into the cause of *Maine*'s destruction. Both authors worked on *How the Battleship Maine Was Destroyed* by Hyman Rickover, entry no. 206. This article continues to support the conclusions in Rickover's book.

191. Hart, Edward. H. *The Authentic Photographic Views of the United States Navy and Scenes of the Ill-fated Maine before and after the Explosion: Group Pictures of Army and Navy Officers. Also, Photographs of the Leading Spanish Men-of-War*. Chicago: W. B. Conkey, 1898. 192 pp.

Photographs taken by a U.S. naval photographer.

192. Haydock, Michael D. "This Means War!" *American History* (February 1998): 42–50, 62–53.

A narrative of events surrounding the destruction of USS *Maine*. The article places the events in their historical context. The courts of inquiry are discussed, but no attempt is made to analyze their findings.

193. Jane, Fred T. "The 'Maine' Disaster and After: The Naval Position of Spain and the United States." *Fortnightly Review* 69 (1898): 640–49.

194. "Last of the Maine: A Fitting Burial at Sea." *Scientific American* 106 (30 March 1912): 288.

   An account of the towing and sinking of the hull of *Maine* off Havana, Cuba.

195. Leupp, F. E. "The Disaster to the Battle-ship 'Maine.'" *Harper's Weekly* 42 (26 February 1898): 193, 196–98, 200.

196. _____. "The 'Maine' Disaster." *Harper's Weekly* 42 (5 March 1898): 220, 222.

197. _____. "Maine Report." *Harper's Weekly* 42 (2 April 1898): 330.

198. Melville, George W. "The Destruction of the Battleship Maine." *North American Review* 193 (1911): 831–49.

   Questions the conclusion that *Maine* was destroyed by an external explosion.

199. Meriwether, Walter Scott. "Remembering the Maine." United States Naval Institute *Proceedings* 74 (1948): 549–61.

   Account, by the correspondent for the *New York Herald* in Havana in 1898, of events surrounding the destruction of USS *Maine* in Havana harbor.

200. _____. "The Unremembered Maine." *Harper's Weekly* 52 (11 July 1908): 10.

   A call to have the wreck of *Maine* raised.

201. Miller, Tom. "Remember the *Maine*: Controversy Continues a Century After the . . . " *Smithsonian* 28 (February 1998): 46–57.

202. Oyen, Arnt. "An Inquiry into the *Maine* Disaster, and Other Incidents Which Were Factors in Bringing about the Spanish-American War." Master's thesis, University of Washington, 1932. 120 pp.

203. Pais, Joseph G. *The Battleship Maine: A Key West Legacy.* Key West, Fla.: Key West Art & Historical Society and U.S. Battleship *Maine* Centennial Commission, 1996. 64 pp.

204. Pérez, Louis A., Jr. "The Meaning of the *Maine*: Causation and the Historiography of the Spanish-American War." *Pacific Historical Review* 58 (1989): 294–322.

Evaluates the various ways historians have used the destruction of *Maine* to explain the coming of the war. Argues that fixation on the battleship *Maine* has served to obscure other explanatory factors.

205. Rea, George Bronson. "The Night of the Explosion in Havana." *Harper's Weekly* 42 (11 July 1898): 221–22.

206. Rickover, Hyman George. *How the Battleship Maine Was Destroyed.* Washington, D.C.: Naval Historical Division, 1976. Reprint. Annapolis, Md.: Naval Institute Press, 1994. 173 pp.

Concludes that *Maine* was not sunk by a mine. Naval Institute Press edition contains a new foreword and an addendum to the appendix summarizing the technical evidence bearing on the ship's destruction.

207. Samuels, Peggy, and Harold Samuels. *Remembering the Maine.* Washington: Smithsonian Institution Press, 1995. 358 pp.

Suggests that *Maine* was destroyed by a mine, planted probably by disaffected Spanish Weyerlites.

208. Sánchez Gavito, Indalecio. *La catástrofe del "Maine."* Mexico: Impr. De L. Bustos de Lara, 1898. 86 pp.

209. Sigsbee, Charles D. "My Story of the 'Maine.'" *Cosmopolitan* 53 (1912): 148–59, 372–83.

210. _____. *The "Maine": An Account of Her Destruction in Havana Harbor.* New York: Century Co., 1899. 270 pp.

211. _____. "Personal Narrative of the Maine." *Century Illustrated Monthly* 57 (1898–1899): 74–97, 241–64, 373–94.

212. Taylor, John M. "Remembering the Maine." *American History Illustrated* 13 (1978): 34–41.

Accepts the conclusions of Hyman Rickover's *How the Battleship Maine Was Destroyed. See* entry no. 206.

213. U.S. Congress. House. *Message from the President of the United States Transmitting the Report of the Naval Court of Inquiry upon the Destruction of the United States Battleship Maine in Havana Harbor, February 15, 1898, Together with the Testimony Taken before the Court.* 55th Cong., 2d sess., 1898. H. Doc. 207. 307 pp.

Official report of the Sampson board of inquiry; includes diagrams and photographs.

214. U.S. Congress. Senate. *Lives Lost by the Sinking of U.S. Battle Ship Maine.* 55th Cong., 2d sess., 1898. S. Doc. 231. 2 pp.

215. Weems, John Edward. *The Fate of the Maine.* New York: Holt, 1958. Reprint. College Station: Texas A&M University Press, 1992. 207 pp.

Includes a list of the officers and crew of USS *Maine* and their fate.

Voyage of USS Oregon

216. Bradford, Richard H. "And *Oregon* Rushed Home." *American Neptune* 36 (1976): 257–65.

 A detailed but undocumented narrative of the battleship's voyage from San Francisco to Florida.

217. Cross, R. *The Log of the Oregon: A Sailor's Story of the Voyage from San Francisco to Santiago in 1898*. Greenfield, Mass.: E. A. Hall, 1914. 60 pp.

 This title is the expanded second edition of R. Cross, *The Voyage of the Oregon from San Francisco to Santiago in 1898, as Told by One of the Crew*. Boston: Merrymount Press, 1908.

218. Eberle, Edward W. "The 'Oregon's' Great Voyage." *Century Illustrated Monthly* 57 (1898–1899): 912–24.

219. Gannon, Joseph C. *The USS Oregon and the Battle of Santiago*. New York: Comet Press Books, 1958. 62 pp.

 Includes a list of officers and crewmen.

220. Shaffer, Ralph E. "The Race of the *Oregon*." *Oregon Historical Quarterly* 76 (1975): 269–98.

221. Sternlicht, Sanford. *McKinley's Bulldog: The Battleship Oregon*. Chicago: Nelson Hall, 1977. 139 pp.

A narrative of the ship's career. Appendices include a description of the ship's characteristics at the time of construction, the ship's officers, and the race around the Horn.

222. Webber, Bert. *Battleship Oregon: Bulldog of the Navy: An Oregon Documentary.* Medford, Oreg.: Webb Research Group, 1994. 141 pp.

Includes a list of officers and crew at the Battle of Santiago de Cuba.

The Opposing Fleets

223. Alden, John Doughty. *The American Steel Navy: A Photographic History of the U.S. Navy from the Introduction of the Steel Hull in 1883 to the Cruise of the Great White Fleet, 1907–1909.* Annapolis, Md.: Naval Institute Press, 1972. Reprint. 1989. 396 pp.

This work includes sections on administration and social history, as well as biographical sketches and technical data of warships.

224. Beehler, W. H. "The United States Navy." Chapter 4, pages 90-122, in *The Naval Annual, 1899.* Edited by T. A. Brassey. Portsmouth, Great Britain: J. Griffin, 1899.

Beehler was an intelligence officer in the U.S. Navy at the time he wrote this essay.

225. De Saint Hubert, Christian, and Carlos Alfaro Zaforteza. "The Spanish Navy of 1898." *Warship International* 17 (1980): 39–60, 110–13; 18 (1981): 262–70.

Lists the ships in the Spanish squadrons overseas during the war and includes a number of photographs. Part 1, "Forces in Cuban Waters"; Part 2, "Admiral Camara's Squadron"; and Part 3, "Spanish Warships in Philippine Waters." A research note describes the official Spanish navy ship classification system in existence in 1898.

226. Dowart, Jeffery Michael. "A Mongrel Fleet: America Buys a Navy to Fight Spain, 1898." *Warship International* 17 (1980): 128–55.

Discusses the important role played by auxiliary vessels purchased by the Navy just prior to and during the war with Spain. Article includes a table of purchased vessels which gives information on the date acquired, original name, new U.S. Navy name, the previous owner, purchase price, and the composition of the ship's battery.

227. Fernández Almagro, Melchor. *Política naval de la España moderna y contemporánea*. Madrid: Instituto de Estudios Politicos, 1944. Reprint. 1946. 281 pp.

Naval policy in Spain from Lepanto to the eve of World War I.

228. *The Flag of President McKinley, Adopted March 30th, 1898*. New York: Vechten Waring, 1898. 16 pp.

A comparison of the navies of the United States and Spain.

229. Grenville, John A. S. "American Naval Preparations for War with Spain, 1896–1898." *Journal of American Studies* 2 (April 1968): 33–47.

Appendices contain the texts of war plans recommended by two special boards appointed by the Secretary of the Navy, the Ramsay plan of 17 December 1896 and the Sicard plan of 30 June 1897.

230. Hannaford, Ebenezer. *The Handy War Book: A New Book of Important and Authentic Information and Statistics . . . with Accurate War Maps and Photographic Pictures of U.S. War Vessels*. Springfield, Ohio: Mast, Crowell & Kirkpatrick, 1898. 80 pp.

231. Harrod, Frederick S. *Manning the New Navy: The Development of a Modern Naval Enlisted Force, 1899–1940*. Westport, Conn.: Greenwood Press, 1978. 276 pp.

   Although this work focuses on the period following the Spanish-American War, a chapter on the Navy from 1865 to 1898 provides some insight into the composition of the enlisted force serving in the war with Spain.

232. Jornadas de Historia Maritima (5th, 1990: Madrid, Spain). *La marina ante el 98.: Antecedentes de un conflicto*. Madrid: Instituto de Historia y Cultural Naval, 1990. 118 pp.

   Two of these five papers delivered at a cycle of conferences held in April 1990 are of particular relevance: "Marinos españoles en su protagonismo historíco" by José Cervera Pery, and "Programs y efectivos navales españoles y norteamericanos (1865–1898)" by Antonio de la Vega.

233. *Naval Vessels of the United States and Spain with Lists and Map*. New York: Mershon, 1898. 32 pp.

234. Rawson, Jonathan. *Our Army and Navy, What You Want to Know about Them: A Description of Our Country's Fighting Forces on Land and Sea*. New York: Rawson & Crawford, 1898. 126 pp.

235. Reilly, John C., Jr., and Robert L. Scheina. *American Battleships, 1886–1923: Predreadnought Design and Construction*. Annapolis, Md.: Naval Institute Press, 1980. 259 pp.

   Heavily illustrated and technical study of early American battleships.

236. Rodríguez González, Agustín Ramón. *Política naval de la restauración (1875–1898)*. Madrid: Editorial San Martin, 1988. 522 pp.

237. Smith, C. McKnight. *The United States Navy, Illustrated: A New Series of Over Fifty Reproductions from Original Photographs and Drawings*. New York: Continent Publishing Co., 1898. 32 pp.

238. U.S. Navy Department. Auxiliary Naval Force. *Report of the Chief of the United States Auxiliary Naval Force to the Assistant Secretary of the Navy on Its Operations during the War with Spain.* Washington, D.C.: Government Printing Office, 1898. 32 pp.

Report of John Russell Bartlett.

239. Wainwright, Richard. "Our Naval Power." United States Naval Institute *Proceedings* 24 (March 1898): 39–87.

A discussion of the naval issues necessary for a strong national defense.

Operations

Pacific Theater

Philippines and Battle of Manila Bay

240. Baclagon, Uldarico S. *Philippine Campaigns*. Manila: Graphic House, 1952. 388 pp.

   A military history of the Philippines, from the Spanish conquest through World War II, with emphasis on the latter war. Relations between the Philippine insurgents and the U.S. military during the Spanish-American War are treated on pp. 58–83 as a prelude to the Filipino war with the United States.

241. "The Battle of Manila Bay: The Destruction of the Spanish Fleet Described by Eye-Witnesses." *Century Illustrated Monthly* 56 (1898): 611–27.

   "Narrative of Colonel George A. Loud," 611–18; "Colonel George B. Loud's Diary, Written during the Battle," 618–20; "Narrative of Dr. Charles P. Kindleberger, Junior Surgeon of the Flag-ship 'Olympia',"620–24; "Narrative of Joel C. Evans, Gunner of the 'Boston,'" 624–27.

242. Beach, Edward L., Sr. "Manila Bay in 1898." United States Naval Institute *Proceedings* 46 (1920): 587–602.

Beach served as a junior officer on board USS *Baltimore*. The article is a description of the campaign for Manila Bay from his perspective.

243. Bell, Chuck, and Arthur Weiss. *Officers and Men at the Battle of Manila Bay, May 1, 1898*. N.p.: Orders and Medals Society of America, 1972. 66 pp.

Lists the officers and crewmen on board each of the U.S. warships at the battle of Manila Bay.

244. Blount, James H. *The American Occupation of the Philippines, 1898–1912*. New York: G. P. Putnam's Sons, 1913. Reprints. New York: Oriole Editions, 1973. Manila: Solar Publishing, 1986. 664 pp.

Manila edition includes an introductory essay by Renato Constantino entitled "Origin of a Myth."

245. Brumby, Thomas Mason. "The Fall of Manila, August 13, 1898." Editied by Willard F. Wight. United States Naval Institute *Proceedings* 86 (August 1960): 88–93.

Brumby was the flag lieutenant on board Dewey's flagship, USS *Olympia*, at Manila. Most of the brief article is the annotated text of a letter from Brumby to his sister written four days after the city's surrender to American forces.

246. Burdett, John C. "The Philippine Expedition: An Episode in the Spanish-American War, 1898." Master's thesis, Louisiana State University and Agricultural and Mechanical College, 1976. 194 pp.

247. Calkins, Carlos Gilman. "Historical and Professional Notes on the Naval Campaign of Manila Bay in 1898." United States Naval Institute *Proceedings* 25 (1899): 267–321.

Calkins served on board USS *Olympia* during the campaign for Manila Bay.

248. Concas y Palau, Víctor María. *Causa instruida por la destrucción de la escuadra de Filipinas y entrega del arsenal de Cavite: escrito y rectificación oral ante el consejo reunido . . . en defensa del comandante de la armada*. Madrid: Establecimieno Tipografico "Sucesores de Rivadeneyra," 1899. 112 pp.

249. Conroy, Robert. *The Battle of Manila Bay: The Spanish-American War in the Philippines*. New York: Macmillan, 1968. 88 pp.

An illustrated, popular account.

250. Dewey, George. *The War with Spain: Operations of the United States Navy on the Asiatic Station*. Washington, D.C.: Government Printing Office, 1900. 70 pp.

Includes Dewey's reports on the Battle of Manila Bay and the investment and fall of Manila, 1 May to 13 August 1898.

251. Ellicott, John M. "Corregidor in 1898." United States Naval Institute *Proceedings* 68 (1942): 638–41.

An account of the surrender of Corregidor following the Battle of Manila Bay. Ellicott served as a lieutenant on board USS *Baltimore* during the campaign for Manila Bay.

252. _____. "The Defenses of Manila Bay." United States Naval Institute *Proceedings* 26 (1900): 279–85.

Describes, in detail, the shore batteries and mines defending Manila Bay in 1898. The article includes diagrams illustrating the range and arc of fire of each battery position.

253. _____. "The Naval Battle of Manila Bay." United States Naval Institute *Proceedings* 26 (1900): 489–514.

This account is based on careful inquiry as well as first-hand observation.

254. _____. "Under a Gallant Captain at Manila in '98." United States Naval Institute *Proceedings* 69 (1943): 33–44.

First person account of the battle and events leading up to it.

255. Elliott, Charles B. *The Philippines to the End of the Military Regime*. Indianapolis, Ind.: Bobbs Merrill, 1917. 541 pp.

See chapter 12, "The Capture of Manila," and chapter 13, "The Peace Protocol and the Treaty of Paris."

256. Farenholt, A. "Incidents of the Voyage of the USS *Charleston* to Manila in 1898." United States Naval Institute *Proceedings* 50 (1924): 753–70.

Farenholt served as a medical officer on board USS *Charleston* during the war with Spain. The article includes an account of the capture of Guam.

257. Fernández, Leandro Heriberto. *The Philippine Republic.* New York: Columbia University Press, 1926. Reprint. New York: AMS Press, 1968. 202 pp.

258. Fiske, Bradley A., "Personal Recollections of the Battle of Manila." *United Service,* 3d ser., 1 (1902): 24–35.

Fiske was navigator of USS *Petrel* in the battle.

259. _____. "Personal Recollections of What Happened in Manila Bay after the Battle." *United Service,* 3d ser., 1 (1902): 202–16, 311–14, 407–20, 536–40, 647–54; 2 (1903): 84–98, 162–86, 225–47.

260. _____. "Why We Won at Manila." *Century Illustrated Monthly* 57 (1898–1899): 127–35.

261. Ford, John D. *An American Cruiser in the East.* New York: A. S. Barnes, 1899. 536 pp.

Ford was a fleet engineer with Dewey. The book contains photos and maps, and discusses the battles of the Yalu River, Cavite, and Manila.

262. Galt, William Wilson. *The Battle of Manila Bay, May First, Eighteen Hundred & Ninety-Eight: An Epic Poem.* Norfolk, Va.: William W. Galt, 1900. 131 pp.

An illustrated historical poem that gives an account of the battle. The book includes a list of officers and crewmen on board each of the U.S. warships at the battle. Dewey endorsed the accuracy of the account in a published letter.

263. George, Jesse. *Our Army and Navy in the Orient: Giving a Full Account of the Operations of the Army and Navy in the Philippines, together with Accurate Detail of the Organization of the Expeditionary Forces, Their Voyage across the Pacific and a Full Account of Spanish Misrule in the Islands.* Manila, Philippines: N.p., 1899. 290 pp.

264. Graves, Ralph. "When a Victory Really Gave Us a New World Order." *Smithsonian* 22 (March 1992): 88–97.

An account of the Battle of Manila Bay, with a focus on George Dewey.

265. Greene, Francis V. "The Capture of Manila." *Century Illustrated Monthly* 57 (1898–1899): 785–91, 915–35.

Greene was a major general in the U.S. Volunteers.

266. Griffin, Appleton Prentiss Clark. *List of Works Relating to American Occupation of the Philippine Islands, 1898–1903.* Washington, D.C.: Government Printing Office, 1905. 100 pp.

267. Halle, Louis J. *The United States Acquires the Philippines: Consensus vs. Reality.* Lanham, Md.: University Press of America, 1985. 57 pp.

268. Harden, Edward W. "Dewey at Manila: Observations and Personal Impressions Derived from a Service with the American Fleet in the Philippines from April, 1898, to October, 1898." *McClure's* 12 (1898–1899): 369–84.

269. Kalaw, Maximo M. *The Development of Philippine Politics, 1872–1920.* Manila, Philippines: Oriental Commercial Co., 1926. Reprinted as *The Development of Philippine Politics.* Metro Manila, Philippines: Solar Publishing Co., [1986]. 489 pp.

270. Kalaw, Teodoro Manguiat. *The Philippine Revolution.* Quezon City: University of the Philippines Press. Kawiliahan: Jorge B. Vargas Filipiniana Foundation, 1969. 335 pp.

A political history of the movement for Filipino independence, with a cursory discussion of the insurgents' relations with U.S. officials during the Spanish-American War. The author takes the position that the United States reneged on assurances made by Dewey to Aquinaldo.

271. Karnow, Stanley. *In Our Image: America's Empire in the Philippines.* New York: Random House, 1989. Reprint. New York: Ballantine Books, 1990. 494 pp.

Includes a discussion of Dewey and his role.

Kelly, David E. See entry no. 470.

272. King, William Nephew. *The Battle of Manila: Or, Dewey's Great Victory*. [New York: Henry J. Pain], 1898. 36 pp.

273. March, Alden. *The History and Conquest of the Philippines and Our Other Island Possessions*. Philadelphia: John C. Wilson, 1899. 498 pp. Reprint. New York: Arno Press, 1970. 485 pp.

274. Merritt, Wesley. "Meeting Dewey in Manila Bay." *Outlook*. 63 (7 October 1899): 313–15.

Merritt commanded the U.S. Army's Eighth Corps in the Philippines. The article provides insight into Army-Navy co-operation.

275. Millet, F. D. *The Expedition to the Philippines*. New York: Harper & Bros., 1899. 275 pp.

Millet was a special correspondent with *Harper's Weekly* and the London *Times*. He arrived in the Philippines with Wesley Merritt and left on 22 September 1898.

276. Motsch, Ernest. *La guerre hispano-américaine aux Philipines, du 21 avril au 16 août 1898*. Paris: R. Chapelot, 1904. 381 pp.

277. Neely, Frank Tennyson. *Fighting in the Philippines: Authentic Original Photographs*. Chicago: F. T. Neely, 1899. 160 pp.

Includes photographs of destroyed Spanish ships and of damage on shore caused by Dewey's bombardment.

278. Nicholson, Grace, comp. *The Battle of Manila: Commodore George Dewey's Famous Victory, May 1, 1898*. Philadelphia: Cyclorama Co., Burk & McFetridge, 1899. 71 pp.

279. Redondo y Godiño, Juan. *Combate naval de Cavite: Impresiónes de un médico*. Madrid: R. Velasco, 1904. 33 pp.

Text of a speech given on 24 December 1903 by the principal Spanish naval doctor at the Battle of Manila Bay, with an emphasis on medical care on board the Spanish fleet during and after the battle.

280. Rodríguez González, Agustín Ramón. "El combate de Cavite." *Historia y vida* 268 (1989–1990): 4–12.

A revisionist account, arguing that the Spanish defeat at Manila Bay was not a foregone conclusion.

281. Sargent, Nathan, ed. *Admiral Dewey and the Manila Campaign.* Washington, D.C.: Naval Historical Foundation, 1947. 128 pp.

Sargent was Dewey's aide after the war, and this narrative was prepared under Dewey's direction. Appendices include the text of original sources used in preparation of the narrative.

282. Sexton, William Thaddeus. *Soldiers in the Sun: An Adventure in Imperialism.* Harrisburg, Pa.: Military Service Publishing Co., 1939. 297 pp.

Dewey's actions in the Far East and the Philippine Insurrection.

283. Silk, C. A., and J. J. Vanderveer. *Spanish-American War, 1898: The U.S.S. Baltimore at the Battle of Manila Bay (Philippine Islands) May 1st, 1898.* Hong Kong: Kelly & Walsh, 1898. 39 pp.

284. Spector, Ronald H. "Who Planned the Attack on Manila Bay?" *Mid-America* 53 (1971): 94–102.

The author concludes that there was no consensus among naval planners on how best to fight a war with Spain.

285. Stokesbury, James L. "Manila Bay: Battle or Execution?" *American History Illustrated* 14 (August 1979): 4–7, 40–47.

286. Storey, Moorfield, and Marcial P. Lichauco. *The Conquest of the Philippines by the United States, 1898–1925.* New York: G. P. Putnam, 1926. Reprint. Freeport, N.Y.: Books for Libraries Press, 1971. 274 pp.

Authors include a discussion of the role played by Dewey's squadron.

287. Torre-Vélez, Juan de Madariaga y Suárez, Conde de. *Defensa del excmo. Señor Don Enrique Sostoa y ordóñez, ex comandante general del arsenal de Cavite, ante el consejo supremo de guerra y marina constituído en consejo reunido en sala de justicia los días 19 y 20 de Septiembre de 1899 para ver y fallar la causa instruida por destrucción de la escuadra de Filipinas y evacuación del arsenal de Cavite.* Madrid: Asilo de Huérfanos de S. C. de Jesus, 1899. 136 pp.

288. U.S. Navy Department. *Correspondence between the Navy Department and Admiral Dewey.* Washington, D.C.: Government Printing Office, 1898. 31 pp.

289. U.S. War Department. Adjutant General's Office. *Military Notes on the Philippines.* Washington, D.C.: Government Printing Office, 1898. 314 pp.

   A guide to Philippine geography.

290. Vivian, Thomas J., ed. *With Dewey at Manila. Being the Plain Story of the Glorious Victory of the U.S. Squadron over the Spanish Fleet, Sunday Morning, 1 May 1898: As Related in Notes and Correspondence of an Officer aboard the Flagship "Olympia."* New York: R. F. Fenno, 1898. 106 pp.

291. White, Douglas. *On to Manila: A True and Concise History of the Philippine Campaigns, Secured while Afloat with Admiral Dewey's Fleet, and in the Field with the 8th U.S. Army Corps.* San Francisco, Calif.: G. Spaulding, 1899. 56 pp.

292. Wisner, J. A., and H. F. Humphrey. *A Brief Description of the Battle of Manila Bay, Sunday, May 1st 1898.* Cavite, Philippines: [St. Clair & Newman], 1898. 21 pp.

293. _____. *Sketches from the Spanish-American War in the Philippine Islands . . . May to August 1898.* [2d ed.] N.p.: Press of U.S.S. *Baltimore*, [1898]. 21 pp.

294. Wood, E. P. "The Battle of Manila Bay." *Century Illustrated Monthly* 57 (1898–1899): 957–58.

   Text of a letter from the commander of USS *Petrel* to Col. George A. Loud, in response to Loud's article on the Battle of Manila Bay, entry no. 241.

295. Zaide, Gregorio F. *The Philippine Revolution.* Rev. ed. Manila, Philippines: Modern Book Co., 1968. 395 pp.

The Capture of Guam

296. Beers, Henry P. *American Naval Occupation and Government of Guam, 1898–1902.* Washington, D.C.: Navy Department, 1944. 76 pp.

297. Cox, Leonard Martin. *The Island of Guam.* Washington, D.C.: Government Printing Office, 1917. 95 pp. Rev. ed., 1926, 82 pp.

   Appendix contains the text of several official documents relating to the capture of Guam by U.S. naval forces.

298. Farrell, Don A. *The Pictorial History of Guam: The Americanization, 1898–1918.* 2d ed. Tamuning, Guam: Micronesia Productions, 1986. 193 pp.

299. Hanks, Carlos C. "When a Cruiser Captured an Island." United States Naval Institute *Proceedings* 58 (1932): 1011–12.

   USS *Charleston* and the capture of Guam.

300. Portusach, Frank [Francisco]. "History of the Capture of Guam by the United States Man-of-War 'Charleston' and Its Transports." United States Naval Institute *Proceedings* 43 (1917): 707–18.

   Portusach was an American merchant on Guam at the time of its capture.

301. Walker, Leslie W. "Guam's Seizure by the United States in 1898." *Pacific Historical Review* 14 (1945): 1–12.

Atlantic and Caribbean Theater

302. *America's War for Humanity Related in Story and Picture, Embracing a Complete History of Cuba's Struggle for Liberty, and the Glorious Heroism of America's Soldiers and Sailors.* New York: N. D. Thompson, 1898. 560 pp.

303. Atkins, John Black. *The War in Cuba. The Experiences of an Englishman with the United States Army.* London: Smith, Elder, & Co., 1899. 291 pp.

Atkins was a British correspondent with the *Manchester Guardian*. The book includes first person accounts of the transport of the expedition from Tampa to Santiago, as well as transportation of supplies to the expedition at Puerto Rico.

304. Bonsal, Stephen. "How the War Began: With the Blockading Fleet off Cuba." *McClure's* 11 (1898): 120–28.

Account of the installation of the Cuban blockade, by a journalist on board the U.S. flagship *New York*.

305. Crosley, W. S. "Some Experiences on a U.S. Naval Tug-Boat." United States Naval Institute *Proceedings* 25 (1899): 65–80.

Crosley commanded the tug boats *Algonquin* and *Leyden* during the war. Based out of Key West, Florida, he operated in Cuban waters and performed a variety of duties.

306. Davis, Richard Harding. *The Cuban and Porto Rican Campaigns.* New York: Charles Scribner's Sons, 1898. Reprint. Freeport, N.Y.: Books for Libraries Press, 1970. 360 pp.

Includes accounts of early naval operations around Cuba, as well as transport of land expeditions to Santiago and Puerto Rico. 116 photographs.

307. Dierks, Jack Cameron. *A Leap to Arms: The Cuban Campaign of 1898.* Philadelphia: J. B. Lippincott, 1970. 240 pp.

308. Doubleday, Russell. *A Gunner Aboard the Yankee: From the Diary of Number Five of the Afterport Gun; The Yarn of the Cruise and Fights of the Naval Reserves in the Spanish-American War.* Edited by H. H. Lewis. New York: Doubleday & McClure; New York: Grosset & Dunlap 1898. 312 pp.

309. Feuer, A. B. *The Spanish-American War at Sea: Naval Action in the Atlantic.* Westport, Conn: Praeger, 1995. 225 pp.

A collection of essays on naval operations based primarily on first person accounts. An appendix provides a list of U.S. ships in commission on 1 July 1898.

310. Gómez Núñez, Severo. *The Spanish-American War: Blockades and Coast Defense* Translated from the Spanish. Washington, D.C.: Government Printing Office, 1899. 120 pp.

Reprinted with seven other essays by the U.S. Navy Department, Office of Naval Intelligence as War Note No. 6 in *Information from Abroad* (Washington, D.C.: Government Printing Office, 1898–1899). Gómez Núñez was captain of artillery at Havana during the war. The essay discusses strategy, maritime law, coast defenses, and naval operations related to the blockade of Cuba.

311. Goode, William A. M. *With Sampson Through the War: Being an Account of the Naval Operations of the North Atlantic Squadron during the Spanish American War of 1898.* New York: Doubleday and McClure, 1899. 307 pp.

Goode was a correspondent for the Associated Press on board Sampson's flagship, USS *New York.* The book contains chapters on specific topics contributed by William T. Sampson, Robley D. Evans, and Chapman C. Todd.

312. Goodrich, Caspar F. "Some Points in Coast-Defence Brought Out by the War with Spain." *United States Naval Institute Proceedings* 27 (1901): 223–46.

Describes the coastal defenses of the United States in detail. Argues that they were adequate to deter the Spanish from attacking any strategic point along the coast.

313. Hemment, John C. *Cannon and Camera: Sea and Land Battles of the Spanish American War in Cuba, Camp Life and the Return of the Soldiers*. New York: D. Appleton, 1898. 282 pp.

314. Henderson, Yandell. *The Cruise of the* Yale. N.p., 1898. 16 pp.

Reprinted from Yale alumni weekly, 29 September 1898.

315. Hernández García, Julio. *La invasión frustrada de los EE.UU.: A Canarias en 1898: el "Tributo en sangre" de 1678–1778*. Santa Cruz de Tenerife, I. Canarias: Centro de la Cultura Popular Canaria, 1984. 60 pp.

316. Hourihan, William J. "The Fleet That Never Was: Commodore John Crittenden Watson and the Eastern Squadron." *American Neptune* 41 (April 1981): 93–109.

Argues that although the Eastern Squadron never deployed for Spain, its existence had an appreciable effect on the military and diplomatic conduct of the war.

317. Jackson, R. H. "Seavey's Island Prison and Its Establishment." *United States Naval Institute Proceedings* 25 (1899): 413–16.

Describes the establishment and conditions of the prisoner of war camp on Seavey's Island at Portsmouth, N.H. Spanish prisoners from Santiago began arriving 18 July 1898 and left 12 September.

318. Jacobsen, Herman. *Sketches from the Spanish-American War*. Washington, D.C.: Government Printing Office, 1899. Reprint. "Sketches from the Spanish-American War." *United States Naval Institute Proceedings* 25 (1899): 11–52, 383–412.

Published in German in the *Marine-Rundschau*, of Berlin, October, November, and December 1898. Reprinted with seven other essays by the U.S. Navy Department, Office of Naval Intelligence as War Notes No. 3 and 4 in *Information from Abroad* (Washington, D.C.: Government Printing Office,

1898–1899). Commander Jacobsen was the commanding officer of the German protected cruiser *Geier*, which was permitted to pass in and out of blockaded ports. The article describes Spanish harbor defenses in Cuba and Puerto Rico and lists the ships that ran the American blockade and their cargo. Jacobsen analyzes the damage done to the Spanish ships at the Battle of Santiago.

319. Kennan, George. *Campaigning in Cuba*. New York: Century Co., 1899; Port Washington, N.Y.: Kennikat Press, 1899. Reprint. 1971. 269 pp.

Kennan, a war correspondent, includes observations of the transport and landing of U.S. Army soldiers in Cuba.

320. King, Charles Brady. *Dedication of the Bronze Tablet at the Brodhead Naval Armory, Detroit, Commemorating the Service of the Officers and Crew of the U.S.S. Yosemite in the Spanish-American War*. [Detroit, Mich.]: N.p., 1948. 15 pp.

321. *Log of the U.S.S. Yosemite*. Detroit, Mich.: John. F. Eby, 1899. 163 pp.

Includes a list of officers and crew and the official report of the action off San Juan, Puerto Rico, on 28 June.

322. Martínez Arango, Felipe. *Cronología crítica de la guerra hispano-cubanoamericana*. Havana, Cuba: N.p., 1950; 2d ed. Santiago de Cuba: Universidad de Oriente, Departmento de Extensión y Relatiónes Cultures, [1960]. 203 pp.

A day-by-day calendar, 1 January to 10 December 1898, of the major events of the war, especially in Cuba, emphasizing the role of the Cuban Liberation Army.

323. Miley, John D. *In Cuba with Shafter*. New York: Charles Scribner's Sons, 1899. 228 pp.

Includes chapters on the transport and disembarkation of troops in Cuba and a table of transport assignments for regiments in the V Corps.

324. Montgomery, J. A. "Sailor's Log off Santiago." United States Naval Institute *Proceedings* 54 (1928): 728–30.

The author served on board USS *New Orleans*.

325. Payne, William C. *The Cruise of the U.S.S. Dixie: Or, On Board with the Maryland Boys in the Spanish-American War: A Narrative.* Washington, D.C.: E. C. Jones, 1899. 80 pp.

326. Placer Cervera, Gustavo. "Importancia de las acciones navales en el teatro Cubano en el desarrollo y desenlace de la guerra del '98." In *1898: Enfoques y perspectivas; simposio internacional de historiadores en torno al 1898, Cuba, España, Estados Unidos, Filipinas y Puerto Rico.* Edited by Luis E. González Vales, 143–58. San Juan, P. R.: Academia Puertorriqueña de la Historia, 1997.

Article provides charts of several naval actions in Cuban waters during the war.

327. Roby, Edward. *The Unfair Treatment of the Admiral and the Captains Who Destroyed the Naval Power of Spain in 1898.* Chicago: Barnard & Miller, 1900. 110 pp.

Reviews the conduct of Rear Admiral Sampson and several commanding officers of the North Atlantic Fleet during the war with Spain to argue that these men (in contrast to Dewey's officers) had not received the recognition they deserved.

328. Rogers, Lincoln A. *Sketch of the Activities of the Auxiliary Cruiser Yale, United States Navy, in Cuban Waters during the Spanish-American War.* Brunswick, Maine: Record Press, 1927. 13 pp.

329. Sampson, William. T. "The Atlantic Fleet in the Spanish War." *Century Illustrated Monthly* 57 (1898–1899): 886–913.

330. *Songs of U.S.S.* Yosemite. Detroit, Mich.: Press of John. F. Eby, 1901. 16 pp.

Includes a list of officers and crew and the official report of the action off San Juan, Puerto Rico, on 28 June.

331. Staunton, S. A. "The Naval Campaign of 1898 in the West Indies." *Harper's New Monthly* 98 (1898–1899): 175–93.

Staunton served in USS *New York* as assistant chief of staff to Rear Admiral Sampson throughout the war.

Minor Actions: Cable Cutting at Cienfuegos; Action at Cardenas

332. Alden, John Douglas. *The Cruise of the U.S.S. Badger, June 5 to October 6, 1898, with the Battalion of the East during the War with Spain: Based on the Log of the Badger.* Asbury Park, N.J.: John D. Alden, 1941. 60 pp.

333. Allen, Gardner Weld. "Two Cruises in War-Time." *Harvard Graduate's Magazine* 39 (December 1930): 163–68.

Recounts service of Harvard graduates, including the author, in the Massachusetts Naval Brigade on board USS *Prairie*.

334. Bernadou, J. B. "The 'Winslow' at Cardenas." *Century Illustrated Monthly* 57 (1898–1899): 698–706.

335. Bonsal, Stephen. "The First Fight on Cuban Soil: The Story of the Landing of the 'First Foot'." *McClure's* 11 (1898): 234–43.

Describes the landing of the first U.S. troops on Cuban soil, 12 May 1898, at Arbolitos Point, by transport steamer *Gussie,* with the fire support of escorts USS *Manning* and USS *Wasp.*

336. Cherpak, Evelyn M. "Cable Cutting at Cienfuegos." United States Naval Institute *Proceedings* 113 (February 1987): 119–22.

Account based on published primary sources supplemented by letters and documents in the Naval War College Naval Historical Collection.

337. Coletta, Paolo Enrico. "Bowman H. McCalla at Guantanamo Bay: A Link in the Chain of Navy-Marine Corps Cooperation." *Shipmate* 41 (June 1978): 25–28.

McCalla commanded USS *Marblehead.*

338. *The Cruise of the U.S.S. Eagle during the Spanish-American War.* Philadelphia: Press of Patterson & White, [1898]. 30 pp.

Published under the auspices of the crew. Includes list of officers and crew.

339. Goodrich, Caspar F. "The 'St. Louis' as a Transport." United States Naval Institute *Proceedings* 25 (1899): 1–9.

St. Louis transported the 3d Illinois Infantry from Hampton Roads to Puerto Rico, 28 July to 2 August 1898. Goodrich was her captain. The article provides the instructions and procedures used in transporting these soldiers efficiently and includes plans showing the placement of berthing spaces.

340. Halsey, William F. "The Last Engagement of the War." United States Naval Institute *Proceedings* 25 (1899): 53–63.

An account of the American attack at Manzanillo, Cuba, on 12 August 1898.

341. Heinl, Robert D., Jr. "How We Got Guantanamo." *American Heritage* 13 (February 1962): 18–21, 94–97.

342. Joy, Henry B. *The U.S.S. Yosemite, Purisma Concepción Incident, June 16th, 1898.* Detroit, Mich.: Privately printed, 1937. 24 pp.

"A defense of Lieutenant Commander Gilbert Wilkes and the crew of the *Yosemite*, in answer to a statement in Stringham's 'The Story of U.S.S. 'Yosemite' in 1898'."

343. McCawley, Charles L. "The Guantanamo Campaign of 1898." *Marine Corps Gazette* 1 (September 1916): 221–42.

An analysis of the campaign from tactical and logistic points of view.

344. McNeal, Herbert P. "How the Navy Won Guantanamo Bay." United States Naval Institute *Proceedings* 79 (1953): 614–19.

This narrative of the campaign argues that the capture of Guantánamo had an effect on the war that far transcended its local consequences.

345. USS *Yankee* Book Committee. *The USS Yankee on the Cuban Blockade, 1898.* New York: USS *Yankee* Book Committee, 1928. 194 pp.

Includes a record of officers and crew with addresses or dates of death.

346. Winslow, Cameron McR. "Cable-Cutting at Cienfuegos." *Century Illustrated Monthly* 57 (1898–99): 708–17.

Search for Cervera's Squadron and Battle and Capture of Santiago

347. "Admiral Cervera's Account of the Battle of Santiago." *American Monthly Review of Reviews* 30 (August 1904): 237–38.

The article concentrates on Admiral Cervera's description of the condition of his fleet before departing for the Caribbean.

348. Archibald, James Francis Jewell. "The Day of the Surrender of Santiago." *Scribner's* 24 (1898): 412–16.

349. Arderius, Francisco. *La escuadra española en Santiago de Cuba: Diario de un testigo.* Barcelona, Spain: Maucci, 1903. 207 pp.

An account of the destruction of the Spanish fleet at Santiago de Cuba, written by an aide on board *Furor* to Fernando Villaamil, who commanded the destroyer flotilla.

350. _____. "The Naval Battle at Santiago." *Living Age* 319 (1923): 548–51.

351. Azoy, Anastasio C. M. *Signal 250: The Sea Fight Off Santiago Bay.* New York: David McKay, 1964. 207 pp.

352. Benjamin, Park. "The Measurements of a Sea Fight." *Independent* 53 (1901): 1833–36.

An analysis of ship movements during the naval Battle of Santiago de Cuba.

353. Bigelow, John, Jr. *Reminiscences of the Santiago Campaign*. New York: Harper & Bros., 1899. 188 pp.

Bigelow was a captain in the 10th U.S. (Colored) Cavalry Regiment. The book discusses conditions on transports and the landing in Cuba.

354. Blue, Victor. "The Sighting of Cervera's Ships." United States Naval Institute *Proceedings* 25 (1899): 586–92.

Lieutenant Blue served on board USS *Suwanee*. He went on shore and reconnoitered Santiago Bay in order to confirm the presence of Cervera's squadron.

355. Buenzle, Fred J. "Collier *Merrimac*." United States Naval Institute *Proceedings* 66 (1940): 1447–53.

Buenzle served on board USS *New York* as a yeoman on Rear Admiral Sampson's staff. His article recounts the preparations made to send *Merrimac* on its mission to block the channel into Santiago Bay.

356. Capehart, E. E. "The Mine Defenses of Santiago Harbor." United States Naval Institute *Proceedings* 24 (1898): 585–604.

Includes photographs and drawings of the devices used by the Spanish.

357. Cassard, William Gilbert. *The Battleship Indiana and Her Part in the Spanish-American War*. New York: Henry C. Taylor, 1899. 146 pp.

   Cassard was the chaplain on board *Indiana*.

358. _____. "Rescuing the Enemy." *Century Illustrated Monthly* 58 (1899): 116–18.

359. Cervera y Topete, Pascual. *The Spanish American War: A Collection of Documents Relative to the Squadron Operations in the West Indies*. Washington, D.C.: Government Printing Office, 1899. 165 pp.

   Reprinted with seven other essays by the U.S. Navy Department, Office of Naval Intelligence as War Note No. 7 in *Information from Abroad* (Washington, D.C.: Government Printing Office, 1898–1899). Cervera commanded the Spanish armored cruiser squadron deployed to the West Indies at the beginning of the war. The documents include internal reports and memos from the squadron as well as telegrams and candid letters to superiors.

360. Chadwick, French Ensor. "The 'New York' at Santiago." *Century Illustrated Monthly* 58 (1899): 111–14.

361. Clark, Charles Edgar. "Note on Cervera's Strategy." *Century Illustrated Monthly* 58 (1899): 103.

   Author's opinion on what Cervera should have done to break out of the blockade of Santiago de Cuba.

362. *Colección de documentos referentes a la escuadra de operaciónes de las antillas ordenados por el almirante Cervera*. 5th ed. Madrid: Editorial Naval, 1986. 276 pp.

363. Concas y Palau, Victor María. *The Squadron of Admiral Cervera*. Washington, D.C.: Government Printing Office, 1900. 117 pp. Translated from the Spanish: *La escuadra del almirante Cervera*. Madrid: San Martin, 1898. Reprint. Málaga, Spain: Editorial Algazara, 1992.

   Reprinted with seven other essays by the U.S. Navy Department, Office of Naval Intelligence as War Note No. 8 in *Information from Abroad* (Washington, D.C.: Government Printing Office, 1898–1899). Captain Concas was the commanding officer of the armored cruiser *Infanta Maria Teresa* and chief of staff of the squadron during the naval Battle of Santiago de Cuba. The essay, a narrative of operations of the Spanish armored cruiser squadron from Concas's perspective, provides candid opinions on the conduct of the war and American treatment of prisoners.

364. Cook, Francis A. "The 'Brooklyn' at Santiago." *Century Illustrated Monthly* 58 (1899): 95–102.

365. Corzo, Isidoro. *El bloqueo de la Habana, cuadros del natural.* Havana, Cuba: Rambla y Bouza, 1905. 277 pp.

   An account of life in Havana during the fifty days of the American blockade of the city. Includes characterization of reactions to news concerning Cervera's squadron.

366. ____. *Cervera y su escuadra: Consideraciónes sobre el desastre de Santiago de Cuba de 3 de julio de 1898.* Havana, Cuba: Tipografía "La Union," 1901. 170 pp.

367. Deignan, Osborn W. "The Sinking of the 'Merrimac' and the Capture and Imprisonment of Hobson and His Men at Santiago." *Frank Leslie's Popular Monthly* 47 (January 1899): 247–71.

   The author was helmsman of *Merrimac.*

368. Dieuaide, T. M. "A Historic Scene on the 'Texas'." *Century Illustrated Monthly* 58 (1899): 118.

   The author, a war correspondent, describes how Captain Philip assembled the crew on deck immediately after the battle to give thanks.

369. Eberle, Edward W. "The 'Oregon' at Santiago." *Century Illustrated Monthly* 58 (1899): 104–11.

370. Eulate Sanjurjo, Carmen. *Eulate, la España heróica y la América magnánima: Estampas de la guerra naval de 1898.* Madrid: Editorial Naval, 1951. 79 pp.

   An account of the Spanish cruiser *Viscaya,* particularly in the Battle of Santiago de Cuba, and of her commander, Antonio Eulate y Fery, written by Eulate's daughter.

371. Evans, Robley D. "The Iowa at Santiago." *Century Illustrated Monthly* 58 (1899): 50–62.

372. Feuer, A. B. *The Santiago Campaign of 1898: A Soldier's View of the Spanish-American War*. Westport, Conn.: Praeger Publishers, 1993. 147 pp.

Includes activities of naval vessels and transports noted by a participant, a private in the 71st New York Volunteer Infantry.

373. _____. "Spanish Fleet Sacrificed at Santiago Harbor." *Military History* (June 1998): 54-60.

A general overview of naval operations in the Caribbean leading up to and including the naval battle on 3 July.

374. _____. "Weaponry." *Military History* (April 1998): 12, 60

The U.S. blockade of Cuba.

375. Fox, Michael A. "Joint Operations at the Campaign of Santiago." Master's thesis, U.S. Army Command & General Staff College, 1994.

Gannon, Joseph C. See entry no. 219.

376. García del Pino, César. *La acción naval de Santiago de Cuba*. Havana, Cuba: Editorial de Ciencias Sociales, 1988. 128 pp.

377. Gómez Núñez, Severo. *La guerra hispano-americana: Santiago de Cuba*. Madrid: Ipr. Del Cuerpo de Artillería, 1901. 242 pp.

378. Goode, William A. M. "The Destruction of Cervera's Fleet. II. As Seen by an Eye-Witness on the 'New York,' Admiral Sampson's Flagship." *McClure's* 11 (1898): 423–32.

See also entry no. 381.

379. _____. "The Inner History of Admiral Sampson's Campaign." *McClure's* 12 (1898–1899): 82–95.

Based on official correspondence of Long, Sampson, and Schley.

380. Gosnell, Harpur Allen. "The Squadron of Admiral Cervera: An Account of the Insurmountable Handicaps Imposed upon a Noble Body of Men." United States Naval Institute *Proceedings* 54 (1928): 651–57.

Describes the materiel problems of the Spanish squadron under Cervera and implies that the Spanish could have done more to increase their chances of survival.

381. Graham, George Edward. "The Destruction of Cervera's Fleet. I. As Seen by an Eye-Witness on the *'Brooklyn,'* Commodore Schley's Flagship." *McClure's* 11 (1898): 403–21.

See also entry no. 378.

382. Müller y Tejeiro, José. *Battles and Capitulation of Santiago De Cuba.* Washington, D.C.: Government Printing Office, 1898. 108 pp. Reprint "Battles and Capitulation of Santiago de Cuba." United States Naval Institute *Proceedings* 25 (March 1899): 81–234.

Reprinted with seven other essays by the U.S. Navy Department, Office of Naval Intelligence as War Note No. 1 in *Information from Abroad* (Washington, D.C.: Government Printing Office, 1898–1899). Müller was second in command of the Spanish naval forces in the Province of Santiago de Cuba. His essay includes a narrative of operations, descriptions and maps of Spanish defenses, and a discussion of logistics.

383. Murphy, Ed. "We Remembered the *Maine.*" Annapolis, Md.: United States Naval Institute *Proceedings* 70 (1944): 55–61.

Murphy served as an enlisted man on board USS *Oregon* after the ship arrived at Key West in May 1898. He was a member of the Illinois Naval Reserves and witnessed the Battle of Santiago de Cuba.

384. Norris, Frank. *The Surrender of Santiago: An Account of the Historic Surrender of Santiago to General Shafter, July 17, 1899.* San Francisco, Calif.: Paul Elder, 1917. 24 pp.

385. Osborn, P. R. "Three Naval Campaigns: A Study in Disaster." United States Naval Institute *Proceedings* 64 (1938): 874–76.

Compares weaknesses in three navies that led to defeat at Trafalgar (1805), Santiago (1898), and Tsushima (1905).

386. Parker, James. *A Review of the Naval Campaign of 1898: In the Pursuit and Destruction of the Spanish Fleet, Commanded by Admiral Cervera.* N.p.: 1900. 64 pp.

A pro-Schley narrative of the hunt for Cervera and U.S. naval operations off Santiago. Parker was a former lieutenant commander in the U.S. Navy.

387. Pérez, Louis A., Jr. "The Siege of Santiago de Cuba, 1898: A View from Within." *Revista interamericana de bibliografía; Inter-American Review of Bibliography* 43 (1993): 633–40.

Anonymous diary, presumably of a British citizen, from 21 May to 7 July 1898. The original is in the papers of G. Creighton Webb at the New York Historical Society. Webb was a U.S. Army officer of the 2d Division, V Corps, who collected materials for a projected history of the Santiago campaign.

388. Pérez de Vargas, Luis. *La opinión y la marina: combate de Santiago.* El Ferrol, Spain: El Correo Gallego, 1898. 27 pp.

389. Philip, John W. "The 'Texas' at Santiago." *Century Illustrated Monthly* 58 (1899): 87–94.

390. Quinlan, Michael, ed. *The Spanish-American War . . .* New York: Published by editor, 1902. Various pagings.

Incorporates the Squadron Bulletins of the North Atlantic Squadron (see entry no. 394) but greatly augments them. The account starts with the blockade off Santiago de Cuba and continues after the war on board the battleship *Kearsarge*. It is completed on board the cruiser *Olympia*.

391. Ramsden, Frederick W. "Diary of the British Consul at Santiago during Hostilities: From May 18, 1898, the Day before the Arrival of the Spanish Fleet, to July 18, the Day after the Americans Took Possession of the City." *McClure's* 11 (1898): 580–90; 12 (1898–1899): 62–70.

392. Risco, Alberto. *La escuadra del almirante Cervera: Narración del combate naval de Santiago de Cuba.* 3d ed. Madrid: Editorial "Razón y fe." 1929. 195 pp.

393. Rodgers, W. L. "A Study of Attacks upon Fortified Harbors: Santiago." United States Naval Institute *Proceedings* 31 (1905): 103–12.

In a series of articles, one section examines the subject of attacks on fortified harbors. Rodgers concludes that strongly defended ports must be taken by the army.

394. Sampson, William T. *Reprint of the Squadron Bulletins of the North Atlantic Squadron.* New York: Doubleday & McClure, 1898. 98 pp.

Collection of bulletins sent out from the flagship to the North Atlantic Squadron to keep men informed of what was occurring in the war.

395. Sargent, Herbert H. *The Campaign of Santiago de Cuba.* 3 vols. Chicago: A. C. McClure, 1907. Reprint. Freeport, N.Y.: Books for Libraries Press, 1970.

Vol. 1 covers the insurrection and early days of the war. Vol. 2 covers major operations. Vol. 3 discusses sieges, capitulations, and the effect the war had on naval and military policy.

396. Shafter, William R. "The Capture of Santiago de Cuba." *Century Illustrated Monthly* 57 (1898–1899): 612–30.

397. "Situation at Santiago de Cuba." *Scientific American* 78 (4 June 1898): 360–61.

398. The Society of the Army of Santiago de Cuba. *The Santiago Campaign: Reminiscences of the Operations for the Capture of Santiago de Cuba in the Spanish American War, June and July 1898.* Richmond, Va.: Williams Printing Co., 1927. 442 pp.

Primarily recollections of army officers; sheds light on activities of transports and naval vessels.

399. *Souvenir of U.S. Gunboat Gloucester and the Battle of Santiago, July 3, 1898.* N.p., 1898. 23 pp.

400. Spector, Ronald H. "The Battle of Santiago." *American History Illustrated* 9 (July 1974): 12–24.

401. "The Story of the Captains: Personal Narratives of the Naval Engagement near Santiago de Cuba, July 3, 1898, by Officers of the American Fleet." *Century Illustrated Monthly* 58 (1899): 50–118.

Also cited separately under each author. See entry nos. 358, 361, 364, 368, 369, 371, 389, 402, and 405.

402. Taylor, Henry C. "The 'Indiana' at Santiago." *Century Illustrated Monthly* 58 (1899): 62–75.

403. *Two Historic Days: Snapshots of Spanish Prisoners from Cervera's Ships Landing at Seavey's Island, Portsmouth Harbor, July, 1898.* Portsmouth, N.H.: Preston of New Hampshire, 1898. 15 pp.

404. Vivian, Thomas J. *The Fall of Santiago.* New York: R. F. Fenno, 1898. 246 pp.

405. Wainwright, Richard. "The 'Gloucester' at Santiago." *Century Illustrated Monthly* 58 (1899): 76–86.

406. "War Time Snap Shots: Photographs that Tell the Story of the Santiago Campaign, with Its Glories and Its Hardships; Some of the Men Who Carried the Stars and Stripes to Victory on Sea and Land." *Munsey's* 20 (October 1898): 3–32.

Webber, Bert. See entry no. 222.

407. Wheeler, Joseph. *The Santiago Campaign, 1898.* New York: Lamson, Wolffe, 1898. Reprints. Freeport, N.Y.: Books for Libraries Press, 1970. Port Washington, N.Y.: Kennikat Press, 1971. 369 pp.

Wheeler commanded the cavalry division in the Santiago campaign.

408. Wilson, Herbert Wrigley. "The Inner History of Cervera's Sortie: General Blanco Responsible for the Disaster." *Journal of the Military Service Institution of the United States* 24 (1899): 463–74.

Puerto Rico

409. Coll y Toste, Cayetano. *La invasión americana en Puerto Rico.* 2d ed. San Juan, P.R.: Isabel Cuchi Coll, 1985. 82 pp.

410. Davis, Richard Harding. "The Battle of San Juan." *Scribner's* 24 (October 1898): 387–403.

411. Hernández, Miguel J. "San Juan under Siege." *Military History* (April 1998): 46–52.

Narrative of Rear Admiral Sampson's attack on 12 May and Major General Miles' campaign to take Puerto Rico in July and August, told mostly from the Spanish perspective.

412. Hernández-Cruz, Juan E. *La invasión de Puerto Rico: Consideraciónes histórico-sociológicas.* San Germán, P.R.: Editorial Xaguey, 1992. 46 pp.

413. Rivero Méndez, Angel. *Crónica de la guerra hispanoamericana en Puerto Rico.* Madrid, Spain: Sucesores de Ryzadeneyra, 1922. 688 pp. Reprint. Río Piedras, P.R.: Editorial Edil, 1972. 362 pp.

414. Rosario Natal, Carmelo. *El 1898 Puertorriqueño en la historiografía: Ensayo y bibliografía crítica.* San Juan, P.R.: Academia Puertorriqueña de la Historia, 1997. 176 pp.

415. _____. *Puerto Rico y la crisis de la guerra hispanoamericana (1895–1898).* Hato Rey, P.R.: Ramallo Bros. Printing Co., 1975. 362 pp. Reprint. P.R.: Editorial Edil, 1989. 336 pp.

Special Subjects

Blacks in the Navy

416. Bond, Horace M. "The Negro in the Armed Forces of the United States prior to World War I." *Journal of Negro Education* 12 (Summer 1943): 268–87.

   Coverage begins with the Revolutionary War and carries through the Spanish-American War, with only a paragraph on the Navy in the latter war.

417. Gatewood, William B., Jr. *Black Americans and the White Man's Burden, 1898–1903.* Urbana: University of Illinois Press, 1975. 352 pp.

   Includes a chapter on the service of African Americans in the Spanish-American War.

418. Nalty, Bernard C. *Strength for the Fight: A History of Black Americans in the Military.* New York: Free Press, 1986. 424 pp.

   See chapters 5, "To Hell with Spain," and 6, "A Great White Fleet."

Diplomatic Relations

419. Bailey, Thomas A. "America's Emergence as a World Power: The Myth and the Verity." *Pacific Historical Review* 30 (1961): 1–16.

The United States emerged as a world power in 1776, not 1898. The latter year was not a sharp break with the past.

420. ____. "Dewey and the Germans at Manila Bay." *American Historical Review* 45 (October 1939): 59–81.

Concludes that friction developed from American misunderstanding of German motives. The German fleet's commander had no intention of interfering with the American blockade, but his insistence on exercising his rights as a neutral "gave a sinister aspect" to his actions.

421. ____. "The United States and Hawaii during the Spanish-American War." *American Historical Review* 36 (1931), 552–60.

Concludes that despite danger of reprisals from Spain for violations of neutrality, the Hawaiian government, in hopes of annexation, rendered every assistance to the U.S. military. The war hastened annexation, which may have been delayed for years without it.

422. Benton, Elbert Jay. *International Law and Diplomacy of the Spanish-American War.* Baltimore, Md.: Johns Hopkins Press, 1908. Reprint. Gloucester, Mass.: P. Smith, 1968. 300 pp.

Provides an American perspective on the relations between the United States and Spain during the Cuban Insurrection and Spanish-American War with an emphasis on international law.

423. Bolton, Grania. "Military Diplomacy and National Liberation: Insurgent-American Relations after the Fall of Manila." *Military Affairs* 36 (1972): 99–104.

American inexperience with national liberation movements and narrow focus on immediate military requirements, rather than on the long-term political picture, led to deterioration of relations and finally war with the Philippine insurgents.

424. Callicott, Wilfred H. *The Caribbean Policy of the United States: 1890–1920.* Baltimore, Md.: Johns Hopkins Press, 1942.

See chapter 2, "Assuming the Burden of Empire: Imperialism through War."

425. Challener, Richard D. *Admirals, Generals and American Foreign Policy, 1898–1914*. Princeton, N.J.: Princeton University Press, 1973. 433 pp.

426. Connor, William P. "Insular Empire: Politics and Strategy in the Pacific Ocean, 1870–1900," Ph.D. diss., Emory University, 1976. 499 pp.

427. Diederichs, Otto von. "A Statement of Events in Manila, May-October, 1898." *Journal of the Royal United Service Institution* 59 (1914): 421–46.

An account by the commanding officer of the German cruiser squadron on the Far Eastern Station. Includes text of correspondence between Dewey and von Diederichs.

428. Dobson, John M. *America's Ascent: The United States Becomes a Great Power, 1880–1914*. DeKalb: Northern Illinois University Press, 1978. 251 pp.

429. _____. *Reticent Expansionism: The Foreign Policy of William McKinley*. Pittsburgh, Pa.: Duquesne University Press, 1988. 216 pp.

Explores the apparent contradiction between McKinley's personal reticence and the dynamic expansion of U.S. influence overseas during his presidency.

430. Ellicott, John M. "The Cold War between Von Diederichs and Dewey in Manila Bay." United States Naval Institute *Proceedings* 81 (1955): 1236–39.

Ellicott served as a lieutenant on board USS *Baltimore* during the campaign for Manila Bay.

431. Ferrara y Marino, Orestes. *The Last Spanish War: Revelations in "Diplomacy."* Translated by William E. Shea. New York: Paisley Press, 1937. 151 pp.

432. Foner, Philip S. *The Spanish-Cuban-American War and the Birth of American Imperialism, 1895–1902*. 2 vols. New York: Monthly Review Press, 1972.

433. Goodrich, W. W. "Questions of International Law Involved in the Spanish War." *American Law Review* 32 (1898): 481–500.

434. Gottschall, Terrell Dean. "Germany and the Spanish-American War: A Case Study of Navalism and Imperialism, 1898." Ph.D. diss., Washington State University, 1981. 164 pp.

435. Gould, Lewis L. *The Spanish-American War and President McKinley*. Lawrence: University Press of Kansas, 1982. 164 pp.

Analyzes how McKinley's policy influenced the coming of the war and its conduct, peace negotiations, and acquisition of territory.

436. Grenville, John A. S. "Diplomacy and War Plans in the United States, 1890-1917." Royal Historical Society. *Transactions*. 5th ser. (1961): 1–21.

437. Grenville, John A. S., and George Berkeley Young. *Politics, Strategy, and American Diplomacy: Studies in Foreign Policy, 1873–1917*. New Haven, Conn.: Yale University Press, 1966. 352 pp.

See especially chapter 9, "The Breakdown of Neutrality: McKinley Goes to War with Spain," and chapter 10, "The Influence of Strategy upon History: The Acquisition of the Philippines."

438. Healy, David F. *Drive to Hegemony: The United States in the Caribbean, 1898–1917*. Madison: University of Wisconsin Press, 1988. 370 pp.

See chapter 3, "War in Cuba and Its Fruits."

439. Laing, E. A. M. "Admiral Dewcy and the Foreign Warships at Manila, 1989." *Mariner's Mirror* 52 (1966): 167–71.

Dewey's relations with foreign naval commanders protecting their nationals and property after the Battle of Manila Bay. Written from the point of view of the senior Royal Navy officer present, Captain Sir Edward Chichester.

440. McCutcheon, John T. "The Battle of Manila Bay." United States Naval Institute *Proceedings* 66 (1940): 843–45.

McCutcheon was a correspondent for the *Chicago Record* on board USS *Olympia* during the campaign for Manila Bay. His article concerns tensions between the Germans and Americans at Manila Bay in the weeks following the battle with the Spanish.

441. Morgan, H. Wayne. *America's Road to Empire: The War with Spain and Overseas Expansion.* New York: John Wiley & Sons, 1965. Reprint. New York: McGraw Hill, 1993. 124 pp.

Discusses the diplomatic and foreign policy goals of the United States during this period. The author argues that U.S. actions were not forced by public opinion but were carefully weighed and motivated by national self-interests.

442. Neale, R. G. *Great Britain and United States Expansion.* East Lansing: Michigan State University Press, 1966. 230 pp.

443. Offner, John L. "The United States and France: Ending the Spanish-American War." *Diplomatic History* 7 (1983): 1–21.

McKinley successfully staved off any European pressure to counter American peace terms. Because McKinley's goals were not incompatible with France's objective of limiting U.S. involvement in the Mediterranean and in Europe in general, the two nations were able to act together to end the Spanish-American War.

444. _____. *An Unwanted War: The Diplomacy of the United States and Spain over Cuba, 1895–1898.* Chapel Hill: University of North Carolina Press, 1992. 306 pp.

445. Ranson, Edward. "British Military and Naval Observers in the Spanish-American War." *Journal of American Studies* 3 (1969): 33–56.

Based on the reports of British military and naval attachés with Spanish and American forces in the Cuban campaign.

446. Reid, Whitelaw. *Making Peace with Spain: The Diary of Whitelaw Reid, September–December, 1898.* Edited by H. Wayne Morgan. Austin: University of Texas Press, 1965. 276 pp.

447. Shippee, Lester Burrell. "Germany and the Spanish American War." *American Historical Review* 30 (1925): 754–77.

Concludes that Germany never had any serious intention of confronting Dewey over the Philippines and that "there was never any real danger of war between the United States and Germany" over the friction between the two fleets at Manila.

448. Spain. Ministerio de Estado. *Disposiciónes de España y de los Estados Unidos referentes á la guerra y declaraciónes de neutralidad.* Madrid: Tipo-litografía de R. Péant, 1898. 131 pp.

Texts of the regulations regarding the maritime rights of neutrals adopted by Spain and the United States, of documents relating to the adhesion of the belligerents to the additional articles (20 October 1868) of the Geneva Convention (22 August 1864), and of the declarations of neutrality of twenty-four countries in Europe, Latin America, Asia, and Africa. Published by royal order of 26 July 1898.

449. Torre del Río, Rosario de la. *Inglaterra y España en 1898.* Madrid: Eudema, 1988. 344 pp.

Treats the diplomatic relations between Spain and England in relation to the Spanish-American War, including topics important to the naval campaigns such as British policy on ships of the belligerent nations in Canadian and other British ports, the passage of Camara's squadron through the Suez Canal, commerce in arms and munitions, use of British telegraph cables by the belligerents, and assistance to Dewey's squadron.

450. U.S. Department of State. *Papers Relating to the Foreign Relations of the United States with Annual Message of the President: Transmitted to Congress, December 5, 1898.* Washington, D.C.: Government Printing Office, 1901. 1,191 pp.

451. U.S. Department of State. *Proclamations and Decrees during the War with Spain.* Washington, D.C.: Government Printing Office, 1899. 100 pp.

Primarily proclamations and decrees of neutrality by various nations, but includes proclamations by President McKinley and decrees of Spain.

452. Wildman, Edwin. "What Dewey Feared in Manila Bay as Revealed by His Letters." *The Forum* 59 (1918): 513–35.

The author, U.S. vice and deputy consul general at Hong Kong in 1898–1899, examines Dewey's concerns about Spanish naval deployments, the activities of Emilio Aguinaldo, and especially the German cruiser squadron. He includes the several letters sent to him by Dewey during the spring and summer of 1898.

Intelligence

453. Dorwart, Jeffery Michael. *The Office of Naval Intelligence: The Birth of America's First Intelligence Agency, 1865–1918.* Annapolis, Md.: Naval Institute Press, 1979. 173 pp.

  Institutional history. Includes coverage of ONI's role in prewar planning and intelligence gathering during the war.

454. Green, James Robert. "The First Sixty Years of the Office of Naval Intelligence." Master's thesis, American University, 1963. 138 pp.

455. McGinty, Patrick Eugene. *"Intelligence and the Spanish American War."* Ph.D. diss., Georgetown University, 1981. Reprint. 2 vols. Ann Arbor, Mich.: University Microfilms International, 1985. 470 pp.

456. Niblack, Albert Parker. *The History and Aims of the Office of Naval Intelligence.* Washington, D.C.: Government Printing Office, 1920. 24 pp.

Marines

457. Burks, Arthur J. "Recall in Cuba." *Leatherneck* 30 (December 1947): 58–59.

  Reminiscences of Col. Enrique Thomas y Thomas, who commanded the Cuban insurgents who cooperated with U.S. forces in the capture of Guantánamo.

458. Butler, Smedley Darlington. *General Smedley Darlington Butler: The Letters of a Leatherneck, 1898–1931.* Edited by Anne Cipriano Venzon. New York: Praeger, 1992. 357 pp.

  Butler arrived in Cuba too late in the campaign to see action.

459. Clifford, John D. "My Memories of Cuba." *Leatherneck* 12 (June 1929): 7, 54–55.

  "Personal recollections of a Marine who was with the First Battalion at Guantánamo in 1898."

460. Collum, Richard S. *History of the United States Marine Corps.* New York: L. R. Hamersly, 1903. 454 pp.

Includes a register of officers, 1798–1903. Also includes letters and reports concerning the Marines in the Spanish-American War.

461. Crane, Stephen. "Marines Signalling under Fire at Guantanamo." *McClure's* 12 (1898–1899): 332–36.

462. Dieckman, Edward A., Sr. "The Saga of Sgt. Maj. John Quick: All Business." *Marine Corps Gazette* 47 (June 1963): 20–24.

Quick was awarded the Medal of Honor for combat heroism at the Battle of Cuzco Wells, Cuba.

463. Ellicott, John M. "Marines at Manila Bay." *Marine Corps Gazette* 39 (May 1953): 54–55.

Recounts service of Marines on board USS *Baltimore,* of whose forecastle division the author had charge.

464. Hanks, Carlos C. "Marines at Playa del Este." United States Naval Institute *Proceedings* 67 (1941): 1591–93.

Narrative of the capture of Guantánamo Bay.

465. Holden-Rhodes, J. F. "The Adventures of Henry Clay Cochrane: 'The Marines Would Stay'." *Marine Corps Gazette* 66 (November 1982): 69–70.

Cochrane was a brigade major at the taking of Guantánamo Bay.

466. _____. "'In Many a Strife . . .'" United States Naval Institute *Proceedings* 110 (November 1984): 78–83.

Narrative of the capture of Guantánamo Bay.

467. Hull, R. R. "Signal Encounter at Guantanamo." *Naval History* 12 (May/June 1998): 18–23.

Describes the important role signaling played in the successful operations of the First Marine Battalion during the war.

468. Keeler, Frank. *The Journal of Frank Keeler, Guantanamo Bay, Cuba, 1898*. Edited by Carolyn A. Tyson. Quantico, Va.: Marine Corps Museum, 1968. 50 pp.

Keeler served as an enlisted man in the First Marine Battalion during the war.

469. Kelly, David E. "The Marine Corps Prepares for War with Spain: The Formation of the 1st Marine Battalion." *Marine Corps Gazette* 82 (March 1998): 64–66.

470. _____. "With Dewey in the Philippines." *Marine Corps Gazette* 82 (April 1998): 66–71.

471. McClellan, Edwin N. "Pages of Marine Corps History: American Marines in Puerto Rico during the Spanish War." *Marines Magazine* 5 (February 1920): 11, 32.

The article consists principally of the official report of First Lieutenant Henry C. Haines, USMC, dated on board USS *Dixie*, Ponce, Puerto Rico, 28 July 1898.

472. Millett, Allan R. *Semper Fidelis: The History of the United States Marine Corps*. New York: Macmillan, 1980. 782 pp. Rev. and enl. New York: Free Press, 1991, 845 pp.

See chapter 5, "The Marine Corps and the New Navy, 1889–1909."

473. Nalty, Bernard C. *The United States Marines in the War with Spain.* Washington, D.C.: Historical Branch, G-3 Division, Headquarters, United States Marine Corps, 1967. 20 pp.

474. Plante, Trevor K. "New Glory to Its Already Gallant Record: The First Marine Battalion in the Spanish-American War." *Prologue: The Journal of the National Archives* 30 (Spring 1998): 21–31.

475. Reber, John J. "Huntington's Battalion Was the Forerunner of Today's FMF." *Marine Corps Gazette* 63 (November 1979): 73–78.

Argues that the Marines' role in the capture of Guantánamo foreshadowed the Marine Corps' new mission in the twentieth century of establishing advanced naval bases, which would lead eventually to the Fleet Marine Force.

476. Schmidt, Hans. *Maverick Marine: General Smedley D. Butler and the Contradictions of American Military History.* Lexington: University Press of Kentucky, 1987. 292 pp.

477. Shulimson, Jack. *The Marine Corps' Search for a Mission, 1880–1898.* Lawrence: University Press of Kansas, 1993. 274 pp.

478. Williams, Dion. "Thirty Years Ago." *Marine Corps Gazette* 13 (March, June 1928): 3–24, 91–111.

Brigadier General Williams, USMC, served as a Marine first lieutenant on board USS *Baltimore* during the war.

Medicine

Farenholt, A. See entry no. 256.

Redondo y Godiño, Juan. See entry no. 279.

479. Robinson, Albert G. *The Hospital Ship in the War with Spain.* N.p., 1898. 12 pp.

   The author was chaplain in the U.S. Army hospital ship *Relief,* which served in the Cuban and Puerto Rican theaters during the war.

480. Senn, Nicholas. *Medico-Surgical Aspects of the Spanish American War.* Chicago: American Medical Association Press, 1900. 379 pp.

   Senn was a lieutenant colonel and chief surgeon, U.S. Volunteers, and chief of operating staff with the Army in the field. This collection of essays includes discussion of hospital ships.

481. _____. *War Correspondence (Hispano-American War): Letters from Dr. Nicholas Senn.* Chicago: American Medical Association Press, 1899. 278 pp.

Young, James Rankin. See entry no. 151.

Naval Leaders and Enlisted Personnel

General

482. Bradford, James C., ed. *Admirals of the New Steel Navy: Making of the American Naval Tradition, 1880-1930*. Annapolis, Md.: Naval Institute Press, 1990. 427 pp.

   Thirteen chapters on as many naval leaders.

483. Challener, Richard D. *Admirals, Generals, and American Foreign Policy, 1898-1914*. Princeton, N.J.: Princeton University Press, 1973. 433 pp.

484. Connecticut. Adjutant-General's Office. *Record of Service of Connecticut Men in the Army, Navy and Marine Corps of the United States in the Spanish-American War, Philippine Insurrection and China Relief Expedition from April 21, 1898 to July 4, 1904*. Hartford, Conn.: Press of the Case, Lockwood & Brainard, Co., 1919. 222 pp.

485. Karsten, Peter. *The Naval Aristocracy: The Golden Age of Annapolis and the Emergence of Modern American Navalism*. New York: Free Press, 1972. 462 pp.

   A sociological portrait of the Navy's officer corps.

486. *A Military Album, Containing over One Thousand Portraits of Commissioned Officers Who Served in the Spanish-American War.* New York: L. R. Hamersly, 1902. 262 pp.

   Almost every photographic portrait has a short caption providing information on the individual's service during the war.

487. Peterson, Clarence Stewart. *Known Military Dead during the Spanish-American War and the Philippine Insurrection, 1898–1901.* St. Augustine, Fla.: Florida Department of Military Affairs, Special Archives Publication Number 146, 1958. 130 pp.

   This publication lists the individual's name, unit, rank, and the date and place of death.

488. Riley, Hugh Ridgely. *Roster of the Soldiers and Sailors Who Served in Organizations from Maryland during the Spanish-American War.* Westminster, Md.: Family Line Publications, 1990. 72 pp.

489. West, Richard Sedgewick, Jr. *Admirals of American Empire: The Combined Story of George Dewey, Alfred Thayer Mahan, Winfield Scott Schley, and William Thomas Sampson.* Indianapolis, Ind.: Bobbs-Merrill, 1948. Reprint. Westport, Conn.: Greenwood Press, 1971. 354 pp.

   Parallel biographies of the war's four most famous U.S. naval officers.

Sampson-Schley Controversy

490. Benjamin, Park. "History and Rear-Admiral Schley." *The Independent* 53 (1901): 1714–16.

   Criticism of treatment of Schley in vol. 3 of Edgar Stanton Maclay's *History of the United States Navy,* entry no. 76.

491. Benjamin, Park. "The Schley Court of Inquiry." *Harper's Weekly* 45 (10 August 1901): 791–93; same article, *The Independent* 53 (1901): 2086–91.

492. "Nauticus." *The Truth about the Schley Case.* Washington, D.C.: Columbus Press, 1902. 79 pp.

   Discusses Schley's actions in the pursuit of Cervera's squadron, the blockade, the Battle of Santiago de Cuba, and the subsequent controversy.

493. Parker, James. *Rear-Admirals Schley, Sampson and Cervera: A Review of the Naval Campaign of 1898, in Pursuit and Destruction of the Spanish Fleet Commanded by Rear-Admiral Pascual Cervera.* New York: Neale Publishing Co., 1910. 333 pp.

The author served as an officer in the U.S. Navy before and during the American Civil War. He was one of the counsels for Rear Admiral Schley during the court of inquiry held in 1903. The book details naval operations around Cuba, particularly those related to the issues examined by the court of inquiry.

494. Rayner, Isidor. *Argument of Hon. Isidor Rayner Before the Court of Inquiry on Behalf of Admiral Winfield Scott Schley.* New York: N.p., 1901. 52 pp.

"An examination of Schley's conduct as the commander of the ship *Brooklyn* in the Santiago Campaign of the Spanish-American War."

495. Schley, Winfield Scott. "Admiral Schley's Own Story." *Cosmopolitan* 52 (1912): 751–60.

496. U.S. Navy Department. *Record of Proceedings of a Court of Inquiry in the Case of Rear-Admiral Winfield S. Schley, U.S. Navy.* 2 vols. Washington, D.C.: Government Printing Office, 1902.

Vol. 2 has over 300 pages of supporting documents.

497. _____. *Sampson-Schley: Official Communications to the United States Senate.* Washington, D.C.: Government Printing Office, 1899. 177 pp.

Includes letters from Secretary of the Navy Winfield S. Schley and Charles Sigsbee regarding the U.S. Senate resolution of 23 January 1899, recommending certain naval officers for advancement. The records used in this debate were important in bringing the Sampson-Schley controversy to public attention.

Brownson, Willard Herbert

498. Brownson, Willard Herbert. *From Frigate to Dreadnought.* Compiled by Caroline Brownson Hart. Sharon, Conn.: King House, 1973. 294 pp.

Brownson commanded USS *Yankee* during the war.

Cervera y Topeta, Pascual

499. [Risco, Alberto]. *Apuntes biográficos de excmo. Sr. almirante D. Pascual Cervera y Topete.* Toledo, Spain: S. Rodríguez, 1920 [1921]. 454 pp., with separately paginated appendices of documents, 75 pp.

Clark, Charles Edgar

500. Clark, Charles Edgar. *My Fifty Years in the Navy.* Boston: Little, Brown, 1917. Reprint. Annapolis, Md.: Naval Institute Press, 1984. 190 pp.

Clark commanded USS *Oregon* during the voyage around Cape Horn and during the war.

Chadwick, French Ensor

501. Coletta, Paolo Enrico. *French Ensor Chadwick: Scholarly Warrior.* Lanham, Md.: University Press of America, 1980. 256 pp.

Chadwick commanded USS *New York* and served as Sampson's chief of staff during the war.

502. Maguire, Doris D. *French Ensor Chadwick: Selected Letters and Papers.* Washington, D.C.: University Press of America 1981. 646 pp.

This book contains four letters Chadwick wrote during the war.

503. Peake, Louis A. "Rear Admiral French Ensor Chadwick: Sailor and Scholar." *West Virginia History* 42 (1980–1981): 75–87.

Coontz, Robert E.

504. Coontz, Robert E. *From the Mississippi to the Sea.* Philadelphia: Dorrance, 1930. 483 pp.

Coontz served in the Pacific as an officer on board USS *Charleston* during the war.

Dewey, George

505. Barrett, John. Ad*miral George Dewey: A Sketch of the Man.* New York: Harper & Bros., 1899. 280 pp.

Barrett, a war correspondent with Dewey during the campaign in the Philippines, takes a thematic approach, discussing Dewey's command relationships, habits, personality, and opinions. Includes a genealogy.

506. Clemons, Will M. *Life of Admiral George Dewey.* New York: Street & Smith, 1899. 196 pp.

A popular account of Dewey's life.

507. Dewey, Adelbert Milton. *The Life and Letters of Admiral Dewey.* Akron, Ohio: Werner, 1899. 559 pp.

Popular authorized biography. Heavily illustrated.

508. _____. *Life of George Dewey, Rear Admiral, U.S.N., and Dewey Family History.* Westfield, Mass: Dewey Publishing Co., 1898. 1,117 pp.

509. Dewey, George. *Autobiography of George Dewey: Admiral of the Navy.* London: Constable; New York: Charles Scribner's Sons, 1913. Reprints. New York: AMS Press, 1969. St. Clair Shores, Mich.: Scholarly Press, 1971. 337 pp. Annapolis, Md.: Naval Institute Press, 1987. 297 pp.

Appendices include select documents related to the 1898 campaign for Manila Bay.

510. Ellis, Edward S. *The Life Story of Admiral Dewey . . . Together with a Complete History of the Philippines and Our War with Aguinaldo.* Philadelphia: N.p., 1899. 448 pp.

511. Halstead, Murat. *The Life and Achievements of Admiral Dewey.* Chicago: Our Publishing Co., 1899. 452 pp.

Heavily illustrated, popular account.

512. Hamm, Margherita Arlinn. *Dewey the Defender: A Life Sketch of America's Great Admiral.* New York: F. Tennyson Neely, 1899. 187 pp.

513. Healy, Laurin Hall, and Luis Kutner. *The Admiral.* Chicago: Ziff-Davis, 1944. 338 pp.

A biography of Admiral George Dewey. Foreword by former Secretary of the Navy Josephus Daniels. Preface by Captain

Leland Lovette and introduction by Admiral Dewey's son, George Goodwin Dewey.

514. Johnson, Rossiter. *The Hero of Manila: Dewey on the Mississippi and the Pacific.* New York: D. Appleton, 1899. 152 pp.

515. Nicholson, Philip Y. "George Dewey and the Expansionists of 1898." *Vermont History* 42 (Summer 1978): 214–27.

516. Roosevelt, Theodore. "Admiral Dewey." *McClure's* 13 (1899): 483–504.

517. Spector, Ronald H. *Admiral of the New Empire: The Life and Career of George Dewey.* Baton Rouge: Louisiana State University Press, 1974. Reprint. Columbia: University of South Carolina Press, 1988. 220 pp.

Critical, scholarly biography that suggests Dewey was more typical of U.S. naval officers in his day than were Mahan, Fiske, or Sims. The author states that Dewey was ill-equipped to handle the political situation in the Philippines after the Battle of Manila Bay.

518. Stickney, Joseph L. *Admiral Dewey at Manila.* Philadelphia: J. H. Moore, 1899. 415 pp.

Stickney, a journalist who volunteered to serve as an aide to Dewey, illustrates the book with many photos.

519. _____. *Life and Glorious Deeds of Admiral Dewey: Including a Thrilling Account of Our Conflicts with the Spaniards and Filipinos in the Orient.* Chicago: C. B. Ayer, 1898. 434 pp.

Includes poems on Dewey and the Philippines.

520. Williams, Henry Llewellyn. *Taking Manila: Or, In the Philippines with Dewey, Giving the Life and Exploits of Admiral George Dewey, U.S.N.* New York: Hurst, 1899. 228 pp.

521. Young, Louis Stanley, and Henry D. Northrup. *Life and Heroic Deeds of Admiral Dewey, Including Battles in the Philippines.* New York: Western W. Wilson; Philadelphia: World Bible House, 1899. 507 pp.

This popular biography focuses on events in the Philippines and U.S. Army operations against Manila and Filipino insurgents.

Emory, William Hensley

522. Gleaves, Albert. *The Life of an American Sailor: Rear Admiral William Hensley Emory, United States Navy.* New York: George H. Doran, 1923. 359 pp.

    Emory commanded USS *Yosemite* during the war.

Evans, Robley Dunglison

523. Evans, Robley D. *A Sailor's Log: Recollections of Forty Years of Naval Life.* New York: D. Appleton, 1901. Reprint. Annapolis, Md.: Naval Institute Press, 1994. 481 pp.

    Evans commanded USS *Iowa* during the war.

524. Falk, Edwin Albert. *Fighting Bob Evans.* Freeport, N.Y.: Books for Libraries Press, 1969. Reprint of 1931 edition. 495 pp.

Fiske, Bradley A.

525. Coletta, Paolo Enrico. *Admiral Bradley A. Fiske and the American Navy.* Lawrence: Regents Press of Kansas, 1979. 306 pp.

    Fiske served as a lieutenant on board the gunboat USS *Petrel* during the Manila campaign.

526. Fiske, Bradley A. *From Midshipman to Rear Admiral.* New York: Century Company, 1919. 694 pp.

527. _____. *War Time in Manila.* Boston: R. G. Badger, 1913. 276 pp.

    Includes Fiske's eye-witness account of the Battle of Manila Bay and subsequent events.

Gridley, Charles Vernon

528. Boslooper, Thomas. "Spanish-American War Correspondence of Captain Charles Vernon Gridley and Harriet Vincent Gridley." *Journal of Erie Studies* 23 (Fall 1994): 5–39.

    In addition to letters from Harriet Gridley to her husband Charles, the article includes transcripts of letters from their son

John and friend William W. Galt. Biographical sketches of both Charles and Harriet provide context for the letters.

529. Schoenfeld, Maxwell P. *Charles Vernon Gridley: A Naval Career.* Erie, Pa.: Erie County Historical Society, 1983. 124 pp.

   Gridley commanded USS *Olympia* during the Battle of Manila Bay.

Hobson, Richmond Pearson

530. Pittman, Walter E., Jr. *Navalist and Progressive: The Life of Richmond P. Hobson.* Manhattan, Kan.: MA/AH Pub., 1981. 235 pp.

   Hobson was a lieutenant and naval constructor assigned to USS *New York*. He led the expedition to sink *Merrimac* in the channel at Santiago de Cuba.

Jones, Harry W.

531. Jones, Harry W. *A Chaplain's Experience Ashore and Afloat: The Texas under Fire.* New York: A. G. Sherwood, 1901. 300 pp.

   Jones served as the chaplain on board USS *Texas* during the war. While this autobiographical account covers the author's prewar experiences, it concentrates on events during the Spanish-American War.

Long, John Davis

532. Long, John Davis. *America of Yesterday: As Reflected in the Journal of John Davis Long.* Edited by L. S. Mayo. Boston: Atlantic Monthly Press, 1923. 250 pp.

   Selections from Long's journal (1845–1915, twenty-four manuscript volumes), with connecting narrative. Long was Secretary of the Navy, 1897–1902.

533. ____. *The Journal of John D. Long.* Edited by Margaret Long. Rindge, N.H.: R. Smith, 1956. 363 pp.

   Selections from Long's journal are more extensive than Mayo's, entry 532.

534. ____. *Papers of John Davis Long, 1897–1904.* Edited by Gardner Weld Allen. Massachusetts Historical Society *Collections,* vol. 78. Boston: Massachusetts Historical Society, 1939. 464 pp.

535. Mraz, Scott R. "Recognition Long Overdue." *Naval History* 12 (May/June 1898): 24-26.

Discusses the working relationship between Secretary Long and Assistant Secretary Theodore Roosevelt, emphasizing the accomplishments of the former.

McCalla, Bowman Hendry

536. Coletta, Paolo Enrico. *Bowman Hendry McCalla: A Fighting Sailor.* Washington, D.C.: University Press of America, 1979. 210 pp.

McCalla commanded USS *Marblehead* and led the cable-cutting expedition at Cienfuegos and the landing of U.S. Marines at Guantánamo Bay.

537. McCalla, Bowman Hendry. *Memoirs of a Naval Career.* 4 vols. Santa Barbara, Calif.: N.p., 1910.

Photocopy of original typescript. Chapters 20–24 in vol. 3 are entitled "The Marblehead in the War with Spain, 1898."

Mahan, Alfred Thayer

538. Mahan, Alfred Thayer. *Letters and Papers of Alfred Thayer Mahan.* Edited by Robert Seager II and Doris D. Maguire. 3 vols. Annapolis, Md.: Naval Institute Press, 1975.

Vol. 2 covers the years 1890–1901. Mahan was a member of the Naval War Board that advised the Secretary of the Navy during the war.

539. Puleston, William D. *The Life and Work of Captain Alfred Thayer Mahan, U.S.N.* New Haven, Conn.: Yale University Press, 1939. 380 pp.

540. Seager, Robert, II. *Alfred Thayer Mahan: The Man and His Letters.* Annapolis, Md.: Naval Institute Press, 1977. 713 pp.

Mannix, Daniel Pratt, III

541. Mannix, Daniel Pratt, III. *The Old Navy.* Edited by Daniel P. Mannix IV. New York: Macmillan, 1983. 294 pp.

Mannix served in the navigator's division on board USS *Indiana* during the war and saw action at the Battle of Santiago.

Montojo, Patricio

542. Pla y Cargol, Joaquin. *Ante opinión y ante la historia: El almirante Montojo.* Madrid: Libreria de Fernando Fe, 1900. 483 pp.

Philip, John Woodward

543. Maclay, Edgar Stanton. *Life and Adventures of "Jack" Philip, Rear Admiral, United States Navy.* New York: Baker & Taylor, 1903. 280 pp.

Philip commanded USS *Texas* during the war.

Remy, George Collier

544. Remy, George C. *The Life and Letters of Rear Admiral George Collier Remy, United States Navy 1841–1928.* 10 vols. Edited by Charles Mason Remy. Washington, D.C., 1937.

This is a bound collection of typed transcripts of letters, newspaper articles, etc., from the commander of the naval station at Key West during the war.

Rodman, Hugh

545. Rodman, Hugh. *Yarns of a Kentucky Admiral.* Indianapolis, Ind.: Bobbs-Merrill, 1927. 320 pp.

Rodman served as an officer on board USS *Raleigh* during the Manila Bay campaign.

Sampson, William T.

546. Gulliver, Louis J. "Sampson and Shafter at Santiago." United States Naval Institute *Proceedings* 65 (1939): 799–806.

Schley, Winfield Scott

547. Schley, Winfield Scott. *Forty-five Years under the Flag.* New York: D. Appleton, 1904. 439 pp.

Schroeder, Seaton

548. Schroeder, Seaton. *A Half Century of Naval Service.* New York: D. Appleton, 1922. 444 pp.

Schroeder was the executive officer of USS *Massachusetts* during the war.

Sims, William S.

549. Morison, Elting. *Admiral Sims and the Modern American Navy.* Boston: Houghton Mifflin, 1942. 548 pp.

As naval attaché in Paris during the war, Sims gathered intelligence on Spanish naval movements.

Sterling, Yates

550. Sterling, Yates. *Sea Duty: The Memoirs of a Fighting Admiral.* New York: G. P. Putnam's Sons, 1939. 309 pp.

Sterling served as an officer on board USS *Dolphin* during the war.

Villaamil, Fernando

551. Serrano Monteavaro, Miguel Ángel. *Fernando Villaamil, una vida entre la mar y el dolor: La guerra de Cuba.* Madrid: Arnao, 1988. 658 pp.

Villaamil commanded the Spanish destroyer squadron at Santiago de Cuba.

Wainwright, Richard

552. Cummings, Damon E. *Admiral Richard Wainwright and the United States Fleet.* Washington, D.C.: Government Printing Office, 1962. 266 pp.

Wainwright commanded USS *Gloucester* during the war.

Wiley, Henry A.

553. Wiley, Henry A. *An Admiral from Texas.* Garden City, N.Y.: Doubleday, Doran & Co., 1934. 322 pp.

Wiley was the executive officer on board the armed lighthouse tender *Maple* on blockade duty off Cuba.

Enlisted Personnel

554. Buenzle, Fred J. *Bluejacket: An Autobiography*. W. W. Norton, 1939. Reprint. Annapolis, Md.: Naval Institute Press, 1986. 346 pp.

   Buenzle was a yeoman assigned to Rear Admiral Sampson during the war.

Gauvreau, Charles F. See entry no. 46.

Keeler, Frank. See entry no. 468.

555. King, George Glenn. *Letters of a Volunteer in the Spanish-American War*. Chicago: Hawkins & Loomis, 1929. 133 pp.

   A volunteer in the Sixth Regiment, King served in Cuba and Puerto Rico. His letters home include descriptions of his experience being transported on board USS *Yale*.

Murphy, Ed. See entry no. 383.

The Press: Journalists, Photographers, and Artists

556. Allen, Douglas. *Frederic Remington and the Spanish-American War*. New York: Crown, 1971. 178 pp.

Includes Frederic Remington's special reports, illustrated articles, and pictures.

557. Bartholomew, Charles L. *Cartoons of the Spanish-American War*. Minneapolis, Minn.: Minneapolis Journal Printing Co., 1899. 160 pp.

558. Bierce, Ambrose. *Skepticism and Dissent: Selected Journalism, 1898-1901*. Edited by Lawrence I. Berkove. Ann Arbor, Mich.: Delmas, 1980. Reprint. Ann Arbor, Mich.: UMI Research Press, 1986. 295 pp.

559. Bowman, Rowland C. *The Tribune Cartoon Book*. 2d ed. Minneapolis, Minn.: *Minneapolis Tribune*, 1898. 92 pp.

560. Brown, Charles Henry. *The Correspondent's War: Journalists in the Spanish-American War*. New York: Scribner, 1967. 478 pp.

The story of correspondents during the war as revealed in their writings.

561. *Cartoons of the War of 1898 with Spain: From Leading Foreign and American Papers.* Chicago: Belford, Middlebrook & Co., 1898. 182 pp.

562. *The Chicago Record's War Stories: By Staff Correspondents in the Field.* Chicago: Chicago Record, 1898. 256 pp.

A collection of journalists' eyewitness reports, illustrated with sketches.

563. Cohen, Stan. *Images of the Spanish-American War, April–August 1898.* Missoula, Mont.: Pictorial Histories Publishing Co., 1997. 392 pp.

Provides a wide range of contemporary illustrations and photographs. Also included are photographs of artifacts, monuments, and historic sites.

564. Davis, Richard Harding. *Adventures and Letters of Richard Harding Davis.* Charles B. Davis, ed. New York: Charles Scribner's Sons, 1917. Reprint. New York: Beekman Publishers, 1974. 417 pp.

See chapter 11, "The Spanish American War."

565. Harrington, Peter. *A Splendid Little War, 1898: The Artists' Perspective: A Centennial Exhibition.* Pennsylvania: Greenhill Books, 1998.

Catalog of an exhibition held at Brown University and four other institutions between 17 April 1998 and 24 October 1999.

566. Hemlandet Company, Chicago. *Hemlandets Krigsbilder från Cuba, Porto Rico och Filippinerna: Jämte Historiska och Geografiska Upplysningar samt Meddelanden från Kriget Mellan Förenta Staterna och Spanien 1898* . . . Chicago: Hemlandet, [1898]. 161 pp.

More than a quarter of the 161 numbered photographs of the war published in this book relate to naval aspects, including Spanish and U.S. naval vessels, life on board ship, harbors and navy yards, and ordnance. Letterpress at foot of page; table of contents in Swedish and English.

567. Méndez Saavedra, Manuel, comp. *1898: La guerra hispanoamericana en caricaturas–the Spanish American War in Cartoons.* San Juan, P.R.: Gráfica Metropolitana, 1992. 197 pp.

Text and captions in English and Spanish.

568. Neely, Frank Tennyson. *Neely's Photographs: Panoramic Views of Cuba, Porto Rico, Manila and the Philippines.* New York: F. T. Neely, 1899. Unpaged.

569. Nelan, Charles. *Cartoons of Our War with Spain.* 2d ed. New York: Frederick A. Stokes, 1898. 59 pp.

570. Paine, Ralph Delahaye. *Roads of Adventure.* Boston: Houghton Mifflin, 1922. 452 pp.

Breezy, personal narrative of a newspaper correspondent who covered the war in Cuba.

571. Russell, Walter. "An Artist with Admiral Sampson's Fleet." *Century Illustrated Monthly* 56 (1898): 573–77.

572. _____. "Incidents of the Cuba Blockade." *Century Illustrated Monthly* 56 (1898): 655–61.

573. Smith, Albert E., with Phil A. Koury. *Two Reels and a Crank.* Garden City, N.Y.: Doubleday, 1952. Reprint. New York: Garland Publishing, 1985. 285 pp.

See chapter 5 for an airy account of the filming of the Cuban campaign by members of the Vitagraph motion picture company.

574. *Through the War by Camera: A Weekly Artfolio of Current Events, on Land and Sea, in the Spanish-American War of 1898.* New York: Pearson Publishing Co., 1898. 300 pp.

575. Wilkerson, Marcus M. *Public Opinion and the Spanish-American War: A Study in War Propaganda.* Baton Rouge: Louisiana State University Press, 1932. Reprint. New York: Russell & Russell, 1967. 141 pp.

Treats the role of the press in creating a climate of opinion in the United States favorable to war with Spain. The author concludes that "the *Maine* disaster may be said to have been the immediate cause of the war with Spain."

Poetry and Music

576. Beard, Alexander Burgess. *The Sinking of the Maine.* Manchester, N.H.: Charles Noll Printer, 1898.

   Broadside. Below the title it reads, "Composed and written during the indecision of the U.S. Government."

577. Brownlee, James Henry, compiler. *War-Time Echoes: Patriotic Poems, Heroic and Pathetic, Humorous and Dialectic, of the Spanish-American War.* Akron, Ohio: Werner, 1898. 209 pp.

578. Bush, Frank A. *"Remember the Maine!": The Lost Ship, Waltz, Song and Refrain.* Belleville, Kan.: [F. A. Bush], 1898.

   Broadside. Words of song in two twelve-line stanzas with four-line refrain beginning, "We'll never forget the sad events of that night."

579. California Club, compiler. *War Poems, 1898.* San Francisco, Calif.: Murdock Press, 1898. 147 pp.

580. Cass, Emma M. *Manila Bay: Souvenir.* N.p.: Prescott, 1899. 10 pp.

   Poetry.

581. Daniels, Cora Linn. *Until We Know.* Wrentham, Mass.: N.p., 1898.

   Broadside. Poem on the battleship *Maine.* Note at the end of the poem reads, "Cora Linn Daniels, Sardia Lodge, Wrentham, Mass., March 1, 1898."

582. Floyd, Annie Earle. *Souvenir of the Present War.* Norfolk, Va.: Norfolk Printing Co. 1898. 14 pp.

   Twelve poems on wartime subjects such as the destruction of *Maine* and the sinking of *Merrimac.*

Galt, William Wilson. See entry no. 262.

583. Hays, Jenny Ward. *The Echo of the* Maine. San Francisco, Calif.: Robbins, Old Soldiers' Printing, 1898. 1 sheet.

   Music with verses included.

584. Mariner's Museum. *The Spanish-American War, 1898: A Semi-Centennial Exhibition–1948*. Newport News, Va.: Mariner's Museum, 1948. 32 pp.

This is a descriptive list of art and artifacts exhibited in 1948.

585. Parker, John A. *America's Great Victories by Land and Sea*. Gardiner, Maine: N.p., 1898.

Broadside. Five poems printed in two columns. *In Remembrance of the Maine, The North and South Combined, Destruction of Cervera's Fleet, Dying Soldier in Cuba*, and *When They Hoist the Starry Banner*.

586. *Souvenir Song Book, 25 Original Songs and Poems*. Manila, Philippines: J. D. Mitchell, 1898. 36 pp.

587. Watson, Moody M. *A Poetical Tribute to Our Heroes Who Fought the Battle of Manila, in Luzon Bay, Sunday, May 1st, 1898*. N.p.: Morsel, 1900. 8 pp.

588. Welch, H. N. *Dewey's Battle in Manila Bay: A Poem*. N.p.: Times Print, 1899. 13 pp.

589. Witherbee, Sidney A., ed. *Spanish-American War Songs: A Complete Collection of Newspaper Verse during the Recent War with Spain*. Detroit, Mich.: Sidney A. Witherbee, 1898. 984 pp.

590. Wolf, Margaret Isabel. *Songs of "Cuba Libre": A Remembrance of the Heroes of the Maine*. N.p.: Lander, 1898. 16 pp.

Young, James Rankin. See entry no. 151.

Consequences, Lessons Learned, and Evaluation of the Navy's Performance

591. Atwater, William F. *"United States Army and Navy Development of Joint Landing Operations, 1898–1942."* Ph.D. diss., Duke University, 1986. 227 pp.

    Chapter 1, "Identifying the Problem, 1898–1919," discusses "the lack of a landing doctrine for the use of large joint Army and Navy landing expeditions."

592. Balfour, Sebastian. *The End of the Spanish Empire, 1898–1923.* Oxford: Clarendon Press, 1997. 269 pp.

    A global account, based on Spanish sources, of the loss of Spain's last old colonies. An important scholarly work that focuses on the disaster for Spain and its domestic repercussions.

593. Birkheimer, William F. "Transportation of Troops by Sea." *Journal of the Military Service Institution of the United States* 23 (1898): 438–46.

Lessons drawn from the experience of transportation of soldiers to the Philippines in a ship named *Ohio* that departed San Francisco on 26 June 1898.

594. Boies, H. M. "The Defense of a Free People, in the Light of the Spanish War." *Journal of the Military Service Institution of the United States* 24 (1899): 15–27.

Argues that Americans should prepare to bear responsibilities as a world power, and should strengthen and reform the Army, Navy, and National Guard, in light of the experience of the Spanish-American War.

595. Clarke, G. S. "The War and Its Lessons." United States Naval Institute *Proceedings* 26 (1900): 127–41.

Primarily a discussion of strategic lessons of the war by a British army officer.

596. Columb, Philip Howard. "The Lessons of the Spanish-American War." *Journal of the Royal United Service Institution* 43 (1899), 420–51.

597. _____. *Naval Warfare: Its Ruling Principles and Practice Historically Treated*. London: W. H. Allen, 1899. 471 pp., plus appendix of 51 pp.

Chapter 20 is an appendix on lessons to be learned from the Spanish-American War. Colomb was a British vice admiral and lecturer on naval strategy and tactics at the Royal Naval College, Greenwich.

598. Concas y Palau, Victor María. *Sobre las enseñanzas de la guerra hispano-americana*. Bilbao, Spain: E. Rodríguez, 1900. 37 pp.

An apology for Spanish naval operations during the war, written in response to criticisms published by foreign pundits, in particular Sr. Bonamico, "Insegnamenti della Guerra Ispano-Americano," in *Revista Maritima Italiana* (October 1900).

599. Darrieus, Gabriel. *War on the Sea, Strategy and Tactics: Basic Principles*. Translated by Philip R. Alger. Annapolis, Md.: United States Naval Institute, 1908. 321 pp. Translation of *La guerre sur mer, stratégie et tactique: la doctrine*. Paris: A. Challeamel, 1907. 465 pp. Also in *War on the Sea, and Extracts from The Genius of*

Naval Warfare, I and II, by Gabriel Darrieus and René Daveluy, translated by Philip R. Alger. Annapolis: United States Naval Institute, 1920. 550 pp.

See chapter 4, "The War between Spain and the United States." Darrieus was professor of naval strategy and tactics at the École supérieure de Guerre de la Marine.

600. Ellicott, John M. *Effect of the Gun Fire of the United States Vessels in the Battle of Manila Bay (May 1, 1898).* Washington, D.C.: Government Printing Office, 1899. 13 pp. Reprint "Effect of Gunfire in the Battle of Manila Bay." United States Naval Institute *Proceedings* 25 (1899): 323–34.

Reprinted with seven other essays by the U.S. Navy Department, Office of Naval Intelligence as War Note No. 5 in *Information from Abroad* (Washington, D.C.: Government Printing Office, 1898–1899). Lieutenant Ellicott served as an intelligence officer on board USS *Baltimore* during the campaign for Manila Bay. The essay describes the actions of each of the Spanish ships during the battle and details the damage done to each one by American gunnery.

601. Gómez Núñez, Severo. *La guerra hispano-americana: Barcos, cañones y fusiles.* Madrid: Ipr. Del Cuerpo de Artillería, 1899. 160 pp.

Includes studies of the effectiveness of naval gunfire.

602. Langley, Harold D. "Windfalls of War." *Naval History* 12 (May/June 1998): 27–31.

Discusses the allocation of bounty and prize money after the war and the effect controversies arising from the practice had on halting monetary awards.

603. Mahan, Alfred Thayer. *Lessons of the War with Spain, and Other Articles.* Boston: Little, Brown, 1899. Reprint. Freeport, N.Y.: Books for Libraries Press, 1970. 320 pp.

Mahan intended that this popular treatment of the lessons would promote an elementary understanding of naval warfare and provide a rallying point for the establishment of sound public opinion on naval matters. Additional articles include, "The Peace Conference and the Moral Aspect of War," "The Relations of the United States to their New Dependencies," "Distinguishing Qualities of Ships of War," and "Current Fallacies upon Naval Subjects."

604. Ortega, José Varela. "Aftermath of Splendid Disaster: Spanish Politics before and after the Spanish American War of 1898." *Journal of Contemporary History* 15 (1980): 317–44.

Includes discussion of mutual influence of domestic politics and naval strategy on each other.

605. Paullin, Charles Oscar. "American Navy in the Orient in Recent Years." Annapolis, Md.: United States Naval Institute *Proceedings* 37 (1911): 1137–76; 38 (1912): 87–116.

See vol. 38, pp. 87–105, "The Spanish-American War in the Philippine Islands, 1898."

606. Roosevelt, Theodore. "Military Preparedness and Unpreparedness." *Journal of the Military Service Institution of the United States* 26 (1900): 58–68.

The U.S. Navy won its battles handily because of years of preparation; the U.S. Army had to overcome unpreparedness "by sheer dogged courage and hard fighting."

607. Santala, Russel D. *Operational Art in the Spanish-American War: An Analysis of the American Way of War in a Major Regional Contingency.* Fort Leavenworth, Kan.: School of Advanced Military Studies, U.S. Army Command and General Staff College, 1994. 53 pp.

Compares the development of operational art and the relative effectiveness in achieving strategic objectives by the U.S. Army and U.S. Navy.

608. U.S. Congress. Senate. *A Treaty of Peace between the United States and Spain.* 55th Cong., 3d sess., 1899. S. Doc. 62.

Also published as U.S. Congress. Senate. *A Treaty of Peace between the United States and Spain. Message from the President of the United States, Transmitting a Treaty of Peace between the United States and Spain: Signed at the City of Paris, on December 10, 1898. Accompanying Papers.* 55th Cong., 3d sess., 1899. [Confidential] Executive B, part 2. 677 pp.

609. U.S. Congress. Senate. *Report of the Commission Appointed by the President to Investigate the Conduct of the War Department in the War with Spain.* 56th Cong., 1st sess., 1900. S. Doc. 221. 8 vols.

Also published as *Report of the Commission Appointed by the President to Investigate the Conduct of the War Department in the War with Spain.* 8 vols. Washington, D.C.: Government Printing Office, 1899.

610. Wainwright, Richard. "The Spanish-American War: Some of the Problems Presented and How They Were Solved." *United Service,* 3d ser., 1 (1902): 1–11.

611. Washburn, H. C. "The War with Spain: A Study of Past Performances." United States Naval Institute *Proceedings* 43 (1917): 1391–1416.

The lessons of war preparedness.

Index of Authors

Note: Numerals refer to numbered items in the bibliography.